Mastering Python for Cross-Platform Applications

Advanced Strategies, Practical Tips, and Real-World Solutions for Building Universal Software

THOMPSON CARTER

Table of Contents

INTRODUCTION

Python has emerged as one of the most versatile and

widely adopted programming languages in the world. Known for its simplicity, readability, and extensive ecosystem, Python is used across multiple domains, including **web development, artificial intelligence, automation, cybersecurity, game development, embedded systems, and cloud computing**. One of Python's most powerful attributes is its ability to run seamlessly across multiple platforms, making it an ideal choice for **cross-platform application development**.

This book, **"Mastering Python for Cross-Platform Applications: Advanced Strategies, Practical Tips, and Real-World Solutions for Building Universal Software,"** is designed to provide a **comprehensive roadmap** for developing Python applications that work consistently across **Windows, macOS, Linux, web browsers, mobile devices, and embedded systems**. Whether you are an aspiring developer, an experienced programmer, or a software architect, this book will equip you with the **best**

21

practices, frameworks, and tools required to build robust, scalable, and efficient cross-platform Python applications.

Why Cross-Platform Development Matters

In today's software landscape, applications are expected to work across multiple devices and operating systems. **Developing separate applications for different platforms** is not only time-consuming but also inefficient in terms of maintenance and resource management. Python, with its **cross-platform capabilities**, allows developers to write code once and deploy it everywhere.

Key advantages of cross-platform development include:

1. **Code Reusability** – Write code once and run it on multiple platforms, reducing development time and maintenance costs.
2. **Wider Audience Reach** – Applications are not limited to a single operating system, maximizing market potential.
3. **Simplified Deployment** – Using **containerization (Docker), cloud services, and platform-independent**

frameworks, deployment across multiple environments becomes seamless.

4. **Consistent User Experience** – Applications behave predictably across different systems, improving user satisfaction.

5. **Cost Efficiency** – Eliminates the need for developing and maintaining separate codebases for each platform.

This book explores **strategies and techniques** to leverage Python's cross-platform strengths, ensuring that applications perform optimally across various environments.

What This Book Covers

This book is structured into ten parts, covering the **entire development lifecycle** of cross-platform Python applications, from **foundational concepts to advanced deployment strategies**.

Part 1: Foundations of Cross-Platform Development

1. **Introduction to Cross-Platform Development with Python** – Understanding OS differences and setting up a universal development environment.

2. **Understanding Python's Versatility** – How Python interacts with different operating systems and the libraries that support cross-platform applications.

3. **Best Practices for Writing Portable Python Code** – Handling file paths, environment variables, and debugging cross-platform issues.

Part 2: Building Cross-Platform Desktop Applications

4. **GUI Frameworks for Cross-Platform Development** – Comparing **Tkinter, PyQt, Kivy, and wxPython** for desktop application development.

5. **Creating Responsive Desktop Applications** – UI/UX principles for cross-platform consistency.

6. **Event-Driven Programming and Threading** – Managing UI events, background tasks, and optimizing performance.

7. **Deploying Cross-Platform Desktop Apps** – Packaging with **PyInstaller, cx_Freeze, and PyOxidizer.**

Part 3: Developing Web-Based Applications with Python

8. **Python for the Web: Backend and Frontend Integration** – Using **Flask, Django, and FastAPI** for cross-platform web applications.

9. **Building Cross-Platform APIs and Microservices** – Designing RESTful and GraphQL APIs.

10. **Creating Progressive Web Applications (PWAs)** – Making web apps feel like native desktop or mobile apps.

Part 4: Python for Mobile Development

11. **Introduction to Mobile Development with Python** – Comparing **Kivy, BeeWare, and PyQt for mobile applications**.

12. **Building Native-Like Apps with Kivy and BeeWare** – Hands-on mobile development.

13. **Deploying Mobile Applications on iOS and Android** – Packaging and publishing apps on Google Play and App Store.

Part 5: Python for Embedded and IoT Applications

14. **Cross-Platform Programming for IoT Devices** – Running Python on **Raspberry Pi and microcontrollers**.
15. **Optimizing Python for Low-Power and Embedded Systems** – Using **MicroPython and CircuitPython**.

Part 6: Python for Game Development

16. **Game Development with Python: Cross-Platform Possibilities** – Using **Pygame, Panda3D, and Godot's Python bindings**.
17. **Building a Simple Cross-Platform Game** – Hands-on project with **performance optimizations**.

Part 7: Scripting and Automation Across Platforms

18. **Python for System Automation and Scripting** – Automating tasks on Windows, macOS, and Linux.
19. **Cross-Platform CLI and Terminal Applications** – Building command-line tools with **argparse, Click, and Typer**.

Part 8: Advanced Topics in Cross-Platform Python Development

20. **Concurrency and Parallelism for High-Performance Applications – Multithreading, multiprocessing, and asyncio**.
21. **Cross-Platform Databases and Data Persistence –** Using **SQLite, PostgreSQL, and NoSQL** databases.
22. **Security Best Practices for Cross-Platform Applications** – Authentication, encryption, and secure coding principles.

Part 9: Testing, Debugging, and Deployment

23. **Cross-Platform Testing Strategies –** Unit testing with **pytest and unittest**, UI testing for desktop and mobile apps.
24. **Debugging Cross-Platform Applications –** Using remote debugging, logging, and performance profiling tools.

Part 10: The Future of Cross-Platform Python Development

26. **Emerging Trends in Cross-Platform Development** – The role of **WebAssembly, AI-powered development, and cloud-based Python apps**.

27. **Final Thoughts and Next Steps** – Recap of key lessons and **resources for continuous learning**.

Who This Book Is For

1. **Beginners** – Those looking to gain a strong foundation in cross-platform development.

2. **Intermediate Developers** – Python developers seeking to build portable applications across multiple environments.

3. **Advanced Programmers** – Professionals working on **enterprise-level applications, IoT, game development, or automation**.

4. **Software Architects and DevOps Engineers** – Those responsible for **deploying and managing Python applications at scale**.

How to Use This Book

1. **Follow Each Chapter in Sequence** – The book progresses from **basic concepts to advanced strategies**, ensuring a structured learning path.

2. **Experiment with the Code Examples** – Every chapter includes **practical code snippets and projects** that reinforce key concepts.

3. **Explore Additional Resources** – Each section includes **further reading materials and tools** for deeper exploration.

4. **Apply Knowledge to Real-World Projects** – The ultimate goal is to **build production-ready cross-platform applications** using Python.

Final Words Before You Begin

Python continues to **expand into new territories**, from **desktop and mobile development** to **cloud computing, AI, and embedded systems**. This book will **empower you with the knowledge and skills** to leverage Python's cross-platform capabilities effectively.

As you embark on this journey, remember that **learning is a continuous process**. Stay engaged with **open-source communities, contribute to projects, and explore new frameworks** to keep up with the evolving world of Python development.

Let's dive in and master Python for cross-platform applications!

Part 1

Foundations of Cross-Platform Development

Chapter 1

Introduction to Cross-Platform Development with Python

Python is one of the most versatile programming languages, allowing developers to create applications that run seamlessly on multiple platforms, including Windows, macOS, Linux, mobile devices, and the web. This capability makes Python an excellent choice for cross-platform development.

In this chapter, we will explore the importance of Python for cross-platform development, examine the differences between various operating systems, and set up a universal development environment to ensure smooth deployment across multiple platforms.

1.1 Why Python for Cross-Platform Development?

Cross-platform development involves writing software that operates consistently on different operating systems without requiring significant modifications. Python is a top choice for this purpose due to several key reasons:

I. Python's Cross-Platform Nature

1. Python is an interpreted language, meaning it does not require separate compilation for different platforms.
2. As long as a Python interpreter is installed on a system, the code runs without modification.
3. This feature makes Python highly portable and ideal for multi-platform applications.

II. Rich Ecosystem of Libraries and Frameworks

1. **GUI Development** – Tkinter (built-in), PyQt/PySide, Kivy, wxPython.
2. **Web Development** – Django, Flask, FastAPI.

3. **Mobile Development** – Kivy, BeeWare.

4. **Game Development** – Pygame, Panda3D.

5. **System Automation** – os, subprocess, pathlib (for system-level operations).

III. Large Developer Community and Support

1. Python has a vast global community that provides documentation, tutorials, and third-party tools.

2. Open-source contributions ensure regular updates and stability.

IV. Strong Integration Capabilities

1. Python can interact with C, C++, Java, .NET, and JavaScript.

2. This makes it an excellent choice for integrating technologies across platforms.

1.2 Understanding OS Differences

Each operating system handles files, system commands, and UI components differently. Understanding these variations is crucial for writing portable Python applications.

I. Differences Between Windows, macOS, and Linux

1. **File Systems**
   - Windows uses backslashes (\) for file paths (e.g., `C:\Users\MyFile.txt`).
   - macOS and Linux use forward slashes (/) (e.g., `/home/user/MyFile.txt`).
   - **Solution**: Use Python's `os.path` and `pathlib` to handle file paths dynamically.

2. **Command-Line Interfaces**
   - Windows uses **Command Prompt (cmd)** and **PowerShell**.
   - macOS and Linux use **Bash, Zsh, or other shells**.
   - **Solution**: Use the `subprocess` module for executing commands in a cross-platform manner.

3. **Permissions and Executable Files**

- o Windows applications often require **Administrator privileges** and use `.exe` files.
- o macOS and Linux use shell scripts (`.sh`) and require execution permissions (`chmod +x`).
- o **Solution**: Manage permissions properly and use virtual environments.

II. Mobile vs. Desktop vs. Web Applications

1. **Mobile applications** have limited resources, touch-friendly interfaces, and often use APIs like Android's JNI or iOS's Objective-C/Swift.
2. **Desktop applications** require integration with OS-native windowing systems.
3. **Web applications** run in browsers and interact with backend APIs.
4. **Solution**: Python offers Kivy and BeeWare for mobile development, and Flask/Django for web applications.

1.3 Setting Up Your Python Environment for Universal Compatibility

Before developing cross-platform applications, it is crucial to set up a development environment that ensures compatibility across multiple systems.

I. Installing Python on Different Platforms

1. Windows Installation

1. Download the latest Python version from python.org.
2. During installation, **select "Add Python to PATH"** to access Python via the command line.
3. Verify the installation:

```sh

python --version
```
2. macOS & Linux Installation

1. macOS includes Python, but often an outdated version. Install the latest version using Homebrew:

sh

```
brew install python
```

2. Linux users can install Python using package managers:

sh

```
sudo apt install python3   # Ubuntu/Debian
sudo dnf install python3   # Fedora
```

3. Managing Python Versions with Pyenv

1. To avoid conflicts with system Python versions, use `pyenv` for version management:

sh

```
curl https://pyenv.run | bash
```

2. Install a specific Python version:

sh

```
pyenv install 3.11.2
pyenv global 3.11.2
```

II. Using Virtual Environments for Cross-Platform Development

Virtual environments help isolate dependencies and prevent conflicts between projects.

1. Creating a Virtual Environment

sh

```
python -m venv myenv
```
2. Activating the Virtual Environment

- **Windows:** myenv\Scripts\activate
- **macOS/Linux:** source myenv/bin/activate

This ensures that dependencies remain consistent across different platforms.

III. Writing Cross-Platform Code from the Start

To ensure portability, follow these best practices:

1. **Use os and pathlib for file paths** instead of hardcoding Windows (C:\) or Linux (/home/).

2. **Use platform module** to detect the OS dynamically:

```python
python

import platform
print(platform.system())        #   Outputs
'Windows', 'Linux', or 'Darwin' (macOS)
```

3. **Avoid OS-specific commands** (e.g., cls for Windows, clear for Linux/macOS). Instead, use:

```python
python

import os
os.system('cls' if os.name == 'nt' else 'clear')
```

4. **Use cross-platform libraries** like subprocess instead of os.system().

5. **Test on multiple platforms** using **Docker, WSL (Windows Subsystem for Linux),** or **cloud-based virtual machines**.

1.4 Summary

In this chapter, we covered:

1. Why Python is a powerful choice for cross-platform development.

2. The differences between operating systems and their impact on Python applications.

3. How to set up a universal Python development environment.

4. Best practices for writing portable Python code.

With this foundation, we are now ready to move on to **Graphical User Interfaces (GUIs) in the next chapter**, where we will explore Python's top GUI frameworks for cross-platform application development. 🚀

Next Chapter Preview: GUI Frameworks for Cross-Platform Development

In the next chapter, we will:

1. Compare GUI frameworks such as Tkinter, PyQt, Kivy, and wxPython.

2. Discuss their advantages and limitations.

3. Build a simple cross-platform GUI application.

Chapter 2

Understanding Python's Versatility

Python's versatility is one of the key reasons it has become a dominant programming language in various fields, including cross-platform development. It can seamlessly interact with different operating systems, support diverse application types, and provide a vast ecosystem of libraries that enhance its portability.

In this chapter, we will explore how Python interacts with different operating systems, examine essential built-in modules that support cross-platform applications, and review the most popular frameworks and libraries for cross-platform development.

2.1 How Python Interacts with Different Operating Systems

Python provides a uniform programming experience across different operating systems. However, under the hood, each

OS has its unique way of handling files, processes, and system commands. Python bridges these differences with built-in modules and platform-independent APIs.

I. Python as a Cross-Platform Language

1. Python's interpreted nature allows it to run on **Windows, macOS, Linux, and mobile operating systems** without needing recompilation.
2. The standard Python interpreter (`CPython`) ensures **consistent behavior across platforms**.
3. Developers can use Python for **desktop, mobile, web, and embedded systems**, making it one of the most adaptable languages available.

II. Detecting the Operating System Dynamically

Python provides several ways to check which OS is running. The `platform` module helps identify the operating system and its version.

Example:

44

```
python

import platform

print("Operating System:", platform.system())  #
Outputs 'Windows', 'Linux', or 'Darwin' (macOS)
print("OS Version:", platform.version())  # Shows
the OS version
print("Machine                  Architecture:",
platform.architecture())  # 32-bit or 64-bit
```

1. Windows returns **"Windows"**.

2. macOS returns **"Darwin"**.

3. Linux returns **"Linux"**.

III. Handling System-Specific Commands

Different operating systems have unique shell commands, but Python provides a way to execute them in a cross-platform manner.

Example: Clearing the terminal screen

```
python

import os
```

```
os.system('cls' if os.name == 'nt' else 'clear')
```

- On Windows, `cls` clears the console.
- On macOS/Linux, `clear` is used.

2.2 Key Built-in Modules That Support Cross-Platform Applications

Python provides several built-in modules that enable developers to write cross-platform applications efficiently. Below are some essential ones:

I. os Module – Interacting with the Operating System

The `os` module allows interaction with the underlying OS, making it essential for cross-platform development.

1. Working with File Paths

Since different operating systems use different file path conventions (\ in Windows, / in macOS/Linux), we use `os.path` for compatibility.

Example: Joining Paths Dynamically

python

```
import os
file_path    =    os.path.join("home",    "user",
"document.txt")  # Works across all OS
print(file_path)
```

2. Fetching Environment Variables

Environment variables differ across OS; os.environ helps
handle them.

python

```
import os
home_dir    =    os.environ.get("HOME")    or
os.environ.get("USERPROFILE")
print("User Home Directory:", home_dir)
```

II. `pathlib` *— Modern Path Handling*

pathlib is a more modern approach to handling file paths,
introduced in Python 3.4.

Example:

python

```
from pathlib import Path
home = Path.home()
print("User Home Directory:", home)
```

III. sys – System-Specific Parameters and Functions

The sys module helps manage system-specific configurations.

Example: Checking Python Version and System Details

```
python
```

```
import sys
print("Python Version:", sys.version)
print("Platform:", sys.platform)
```

IV. shutil – High-Level File and Directory Operations

The shutil module provides functions to handle file operations such as copying, moving, and removing files.

Example: Copying a File Across Platforms

```
python
```

```
import shutil
shutil.copy("source.txt", "destination.txt")    #
Works on Windows, macOS, and Linux
```

V. *subprocess* – *Running External Commands*

Instead of `os.system()`, `subprocess` is a better approach for running shell commands.

Example: Running a Cross-Platform Command

```
python
```

```
import subprocess
result    =    subprocess.run(["echo",    "Hello,
World!"], capture_output=True, text=True)
print(result.stdout)
```

This ensures compatibility across Windows, macOS, and Linux.

2.3 Popular Frameworks and Libraries for Cross-Platform Development

Python's ecosystem includes several robust frameworks and libraries designed specifically for cross-platform application development. Below are some of the most widely used ones:

I. GUI Development

1. **Tkinter** – Built into Python, lightweight for basic GUIs.
2. **PyQt/PySide** – Feature-rich UI development using Qt.
3. **Kivy** – Best for mobile and touch-based apps.
4. **wxPython** – Native-looking desktop apps for Windows, macOS, and Linux.

II. Web Development

1. **Django** – Full-stack web framework.
2. **Flask** – Lightweight and flexible.
3. **FastAPI** – Optimized for speed and modern web APIs.

III. Mobile Development

1. **Kivy** – Used for mobile apps on Android and iOS.

2. **BeeWare** – Converts Python code into native iOS and Android applications.

IV. Game Development

1. **Pygame** – Used for 2D game development.
2. **Panda3D** – Advanced game engine.
3. **Godot (GDScript + Python Bindings)** – Open-source game engine.

V. Automation and Scripting

1. **Ansible** – Automates IT operations.
2. **Fabric** – Automates remote server management.
3. **PyAutoGUI** – Automates GUI tasks across platforms.

VI. Machine Learning & Data Science

1. **TensorFlow & PyTorch** – AI and ML development.
2. **Pandas & NumPy** – Data processing and analysis.
3. **Matplotlib & Seaborn** – Data visualization.

51

2.4 Summary

In this chapter, we explored:

1. How Python interacts with different operating systems using built-in modules like os, sys, and pathlib.
2. Essential Python modules for handling system commands, file management, and OS detection.
3. A comprehensive list of frameworks and libraries that enable cross-platform application development in GUI, web, mobile, automation, and game development.

By leveraging Python's extensive built-in features and third-party libraries, developers can write code that runs seamlessly across different environments.

Next Chapter Preview: Best Practices for Writing Portable Python Code

In the next chapter, we will:

1. Learn how to structure Python code for maximum portability.

2. Handle dependencies using virtual environments and package managers.

3. Write robust, maintainable, and scalable cross-platform applications.

Chapter 3

Best Practices for Writing Portable Python Code

Writing portable Python code ensures that your applications run smoothly across multiple operating systems without requiring modifications. By following best practices, handling OS-specific differences, and debugging cross-platform issues effectively, developers can build robust and maintainable software.

In this chapter, we will explore key coding conventions, techniques for handling file systems and environment variables, and strategies for debugging cross-platform compatibility issues.

3.1 Coding Conventions for Portability

Following proper coding conventions enhances the readability, maintainability, and cross-platform compatibility of your Python code.

I. Use a Consistent Code Style

1. Follow the **PEP 8** style guide to maintain code consistency.
2. Use clear variable and function names to enhance readability.
3. Keep indentation consistent (preferably **4 spaces per indentation level**).

Example:

```python

def read_file(file_path):
    """Reads and returns the content of a file."""
    with open(file_path, "r", encoding="utf-8") as file:
        return file.read()
```

II. Avoid Hardcoding Platform-Specific Paths

1. Avoid using platform-dependent file paths like `C:\Users\Documents\file.txt`.

2. Instead, use `os.path` or `pathlib` to construct file paths dynamically.

Example: Using `pathlib` for Cross-Platform Path Handling

```python
python

from pathlib import Path

# Define a universal file path
file_path   =   Path.home()   /   "Documents"   /
"file.txt"
print(file_path)
```

- This method works on **Windows, macOS, and Linux** without modification.

III. Write Python 3 Compatible Code

1. Always use **Python 3+** to leverage modern features and avoid deprecated methods.
2. Avoid Python 2-specific functions, such as `print "Hello"` (use `print("Hello")`).

IV. Prefer Standard Libraries Over OS-Specific Solutions

1. Instead of system commands (`os.system()`), use Python's built-in modules like `shutil`, `subprocess`, and `pathlib`.

2. **Example: Using `shutil` instead of OS commands**

```python
python

import shutil
shutil.copy("source.txt",
"destination.txt")  # Works on all OS
```

3.2 Handling Path Differences, File Systems, and Environment Variables

Each operating system has a different way of handling file paths, system directories, and environment variables. Using the correct approach ensures your Python scripts function correctly across platforms.

I. Handling File Paths Correctly

1. Windows vs. macOS/Linux Path Differences

1. **Windows** uses backslashes (\) in file paths.
2. **macOS/Linux** use forward slashes (/).

Solution: Use `os.path` or `pathlib` for compatibility.

```python
```

```python
import os
file_path = os.path.join("folder", "subfolder",
"file.txt")  # Works on all OS
```

Better: Use `pathlib` for cleaner code

```python
```

```python
from pathlib import Path
file_path  =  Path("folder")  /  "subfolder"  /
"file.txt"
```

II. Managing Environment Variables

Environment variables store important configuration settings that vary by OS.

1. Setting and Retrieving Environment Variables

Windows (Command Prompt):

```sh
```

```sh
set API_KEY=123456
```

Linux/macOS (Terminal):

```sh
```

```sh
export API_KEY=123456
```

Accessing Environment Variables in Python

```python
```

```python
import os
api_key = os.getenv("API_KEY", "default_value")
print(api_key)
```

III. Handling File Encoding Issues

Different operating systems use different default encodings, which can cause issues when reading/writing files.

Solution: Always specify UTF-8 encoding

59

```python
with open("file.txt", "r", encoding="utf-8") as
file:
    content = file.read()
```

3.3 Debugging Cross-Platform Issues Effectively

Debugging cross-platform issues requires testing on multiple operating systems and identifying potential points of failure.

I. Testing Across Multiple Operating Systems

1. **Test on Windows, macOS, and Linux** before deploying your application.
2. Use **Docker** or **WSL (Windows Subsystem for Linux)** to test Linux environments on a Windows machine.
3. Use **virtual machines (VMs)** or cloud-based services like **GitHub Actions** or **Travis CI** for automated testing.

II. Identifying and Fixing Cross-Platform Bugs

1. Check OS-Specific Issues with `platform` *Module*

python

```
import platform
if platform.system() == "Windows":
    print("Running on Windows")
elif platform.system() == "Linux":
    print("Running on Linux")
elif platform.system() == "Darwin":   # macOS
    print("Running on macOS")
```

III. Using Logging for Debugging

Instead of `print()` statements, use `logging` to capture debugging information.

Example: Implementing Logging in a Cross-Platform Application

python

```
import logging
```

61

```
# Configure logging
logging.basicConfig(level=logging.DEBUG,
format="%(asctime)s    -    %(levelname)s    -
%(message)s")

# Sample debug message
logging.debug("Debugging message for testing.")
```

IV. Using Automated Testing for Cross-Platform Compatibility

1. Write Unit Tests with pytest

```python
import pytest

def add(a, b):
    return a + b

def test_add():
    assert add(2, 3) == 5
```

Run tests with:

```sh
```

```
pytest test_script.py
```

2. Use CI/CD Pipelines for Multi-Platform Testing

- **GitHub Actions** can test on Windows, macOS, and Linux automatically.
- **Example** `.github/workflows/python-ci.yml`:

yaml

```yaml
name: Python Cross-Platform Tests

on: [push]

jobs:
  test:
    strategy:
      matrix:
        os: [ubuntu-latest, macos-latest, windows-latest]
    runs-on: ${{ matrix.os }}

    steps:
    - uses: actions/checkout@v2
    - name: Set up Python
      uses: actions/setup-python@v2
      with:
        python-version: '3.x'
    - name: Install dependencies
```

```
    run: pip install pytest
  - name: Run tests
    run: pytest
```

This ensures that the code runs correctly on all major operating systems before deployment.

3.4 Summary

In this chapter, we covered:

1. Best coding practices for writing portable Python code.
2. Handling OS-specific path differences, file systems, and environment variables.
3. Debugging strategies for identifying and fixing cross-platform issues.
4. Using logging, unit testing, and CI/CD pipelines to ensure cross-platform compatibility.

By following these best practices, developers can write Python applications that work seamlessly across Windows, macOS, Linux, and other environments.

Next Chapter Preview: GUI Frameworks for Cross-Platform Development

In the next chapter, we will:

1. Compare cross-platform GUI frameworks such as Tkinter, PyQt, Kivy, and wxPython.
2. Learn their advantages, limitations, and best use cases.
3. Build a simple GUI application that works across different platforms.

Chapter 4

GUI Frameworks for Cross-Platform Development

Graphical User Interfaces (GUIs) allow users to interact with applications visually, making software more intuitive and user-friendly. Python provides several powerful frameworks for developing cross-platform desktop applications, ensuring compatibility with Windows, macOS, and Linux.

In this chapter, we will explore four popular GUI frameworks—**Tkinter, PyQt/PySide, Kivy, and wxPython**—comparing their strengths, weaknesses, and best use cases.

4.1 Comparing Tkinter, PyQt/PySide, Kivy, and wxPython

Python offers multiple GUI frameworks, each with unique capabilities. Below is a high-level comparison:

Framework	Platform Support	Best For	Difficulty Level	Look & Feel
Tkinter	Windows, macOS, Linux	Simple desktop apps	Easy	Basic, outdated
PyQt/PySide	Windows, macOS, Linux	Complex, modern applications	Moderate	Native & customizable
Kivy	Windows, macOS, Linux, iOS, Android	Touch-based & mobile apps	Difficult	Custom (not native)
wxPython	Windows, macOS, Linux	Native-looking desktop apps	Moderate	Native appearance

4.2 Strengths and Weaknesses of Each Framework

I. Tkinter: The Built-in Lightweight GUI Toolkit

1. Overview

Tkinter is the **default GUI framework** bundled with Python. It is lightweight, easy to use, and requires no additional installations.

2. Strengths

1. **Built-in** – Comes with Python, no need for separate installation.
2. **Simple and easy to learn** – Ideal for small-scale applications.
3. **Lightweight** – Fast and efficient for basic GUIs.

3. Weaknesses

1. **Limited widgets** – Lacks advanced UI elements like grids, toolbars, and complex layouts.

2. **Outdated appearance** – The UI looks dated compared to modern toolkits.

3. **Not ideal for large applications** – Managing large-scale applications can be difficult.

4. Example: Simple Tkinter Window

python

```
import tkinter as tk

root = tk.Tk()
root.title("Tkinter Example")
root.geometry("300x200")

label = tk.Label(root, text="Hello, Tkinter!")
label.pack()

root.mainloop()
```

Best for: Small GUI applications, beginners, quick prototypes.

II. PyQt / PySide: Feature-Rich, Modern UI Development

1. Overview

PyQt and PySide are Python bindings for the **Qt framework**, which powers many modern applications. PyQt and PySide offer nearly identical functionality, but PyQt uses a commercial license, while PySide is LGPL (free for commercial use).

2. Strengths

1. **Modern and polished UI** – Looks native on Windows, macOS, and Linux.
2. **Advanced features** – Includes widgets, animations, drag-and-drop, and styling with **Qt Stylesheets**.
3. **Large community support** – Well-documented and widely used in industry.

3. Weaknesses

1. **Steeper learning curve** – Requires learning Qt concepts like signals and slots.
2. **Larger installation size** – Heavier than Tkinter.
3. **Commercial licensing for PyQt** – PyQt requires a paid license for commercial projects, while PySide does not.

4. Example: Simple PyQt Window

```python
python
```

```
from    PyQt6.QtWidgets    import    QApplication,
QLabel, QWidget

app = QApplication([])
window = QWidget()
window.setWindowTitle("PyQt Example")
label = QLabel("Hello, PyQt!", parent=window)
window.show()
app.exec()
```

Best for: Complex, modern-looking desktop applications.

III. Kivy: Best for Mobile and Touch-Based Applications

1. Overview

Kivy is a **cross-platform GUI framework** that supports Windows, macOS, Linux, iOS, and Android. It is optimized for touch-based applications and is commonly used in mobile development.

2. Strengths

1. **Multi-touch support** – Ideal for mobile and tablet applications.
2. **Supports multiple platforms** – Works on **desktop and mobile (Android & iOS)**.
3. **Highly customizable UI** – Uses KV language for declarative UI design.

3. Weaknesses

1. **Non-native look** – UI elements do not look like standard OS elements.
2. **Complex setup for mobile** – Deploying on Android and iOS requires additional dependencies.
3. **Steeper learning curve** – Requires learning KV language.

4. Example: Simple Kivy App

python

```python
from kivy.app import App
from kivy.uix.label import Label

class MyApp(App):
    def build(self):
        return Label(text="Hello, Kivy!")

MyApp().run()
```

Best for: Mobile apps, touch-based applications, modern interactive UI.

IV. wxPython: Native-Looking GUI for Desktop Applications

1. Overview

wxPython is a Python wrapper for **wxWidgets**, a GUI library that provides native-looking applications on Windows, macOS, and Linux.

2. Strengths

1. **Native look and feel** – Uses native OS widgets, making apps blend seamlessly.
2. **Rich widget set** – Supports advanced UI components.
3. **Good performance** – Faster than Tkinter for complex applications.

3. Weaknesses

1. **Limited documentation** – Harder to find resources compared to PyQt.

2. **Not as widely used** – Smaller community compared to PyQt/Kivy.

3. **Complex event handling** – Uses event-driven programming, which can be tricky.

4. Example: Simple wxPython App

python

```
import wx

app = wx.App(False)
frame  =  wx.Frame(None,  wx.ID_ANY,  "wxPython
Example")
frame.Show()
app.MainLoop()
```

Best for: Desktop applications that require a native appearance and feel.

4.3 Summary: Choosing the Right GUI Framework

Framework	Best For	Pros	Cons
Tkinter	Simple desktop apps	Built-in, lightweight, easy to learn	Outdated look, limited widgets
PyQt/PySide	Modern, feature-rich apps	Customizable, powerful UI, supports animations	Steep learning curve, larger install
Kivy	Mobile & touch apps	Multi-touch support, works on Android/iOS	Non-native look, complex setup
wxPython	Native-looking desktop apps	Fast, uses native OS elements	Smaller community, tricky event handling

How to Choose the Right Framework:

1. If you need a **quick and simple GUI**, use **Tkinter**.

75

2. If you want a **modern desktop app**, use **PyQt/PySide**.

3. If you need **mobile support or touch-based apps**, use **Kivy**.

4. If you need a **native-looking desktop app**, use **wxPython**.

Next Chapter Preview: Creating Responsive Desktop Applications

In the next chapter, we will:

1. Learn **how to design a GUI layout that adapts to different screen sizes**.

2. Implement **responsive design techniques in PyQt, Kivy, and wxPython**.

3. Ensure UI consistency across different operating systems.

Part 2

Building Cross-Platform Desktop Applications

Chapter 5

Creating Responsive Desktop Applications

Building **responsive desktop applications** ensures that your UI adapts dynamically to different screen sizes, resolutions, and operating systems. Since users may run your application on various displays, from small laptops to ultra-wide monitors, designing a UI that maintains consistency and usability across platforms is essential.

In this chapter, we will cover:

1. **UI/UX principles** for maintaining cross-platform consistency.
2. **Techniques for writing adaptive layouts** that work on different screen resolutions.

5.1 UI/UX Principles for Cross-Platform Consistency

A well-designed UI provides a seamless experience across operating systems. The following principles ensure **consistency, usability, and adaptability** in your cross-platform application.

I. Use Platform-Native Design Guidelines

1. **Windows** follows the **Fluent Design System** (with transparency, depth, and animation).
2. **macOS** adheres to **Human Interface Guidelines (HIG)** (rounded edges, smooth transitions).
3. **Linux** varies, but GNOME and KDE desktops prefer **clean, functional UI layouts**.

Solution: Follow UI standards that match user expectations for each OS.

II. Maintain a Minimal and Intuitive Layout

1. **Prioritize usability** – Avoid cluttered interfaces.
2. **Use clear typography** – Choose legible fonts (`Arial`, `Roboto`, `Segoe UI`).
3. **Ensure accessibility** – Support high-contrast themes and screen readers.

Solution: Keep UI **simple, clear, and functional**, using recognizable icons and buttons.

III. Support Multiple Screen Sizes and Resolutions

1. Avoid **fixed-size** UI elements – they may not scale properly on high-DPI screens.
2. Use **relative sizing** (percentages, flexible layouts) instead of fixed pixel values.
3. Implement **adaptive design techniques** to optimize content for different resolutions.

Solution: Use **grid layouts, auto-scaling elements, and viewport detection** to adjust UI dynamically.

IV. Use Cross-Platform Fonts and Colors

Fonts and colors should look consistent across operating systems.

1. Use **standard fonts** available on all platforms:
    o   Windows: `Segoe UI`
    o   macOS: `San Francisco`
    o   Linux: `Ubuntu Font`
2. Define **color schemes** that work well in light and dark modes.

Solution: Let the **system theme dictate UI colors** for consistency.

5.2 Writing Adaptive Layouts for Different Screen Resolutions

A **responsive UI** dynamically adjusts its layout based on screen size, DPI scaling, and user preferences.

I. Using Grid Layouts for Flexible UIs

Instead of **fixed positioning**, use **grid-based** or **flexbox-like** layouts.

Example: Using PyQt's `QGridLayout`

python

```python
from PyQt6.QtWidgets import QApplication, QWidget, QLabel, QGridLayout

app = QApplication([])
window = QWidget()
layout = QGridLayout()

label1 = QLabel("Top Left")
label2 = QLabel("Top Right")
label3 = QLabel("Bottom Left")
```

```
label4 = QLabel("Bottom Right")

layout.addWidget(label1, 0, 0)
layout.addWidget(label2, 0, 1)
layout.addWidget(label3, 1, 0)
layout.addWidget(label4, 1, 1)

window.setLayout(layout)
window.show()
app.exec()
```

- The **grid layout** ensures the UI scales properly.
- Elements adjust based on the **window size and available space**.

Best for: Dynamic UIs that need **consistent resizing** behavior.

II. Using Box Layouts for Auto-Scaling UIs

Box layouts automatically adjust UI components when the window resizes.

Example: Using PyQt's `QVBoxLayout` (Vertical Layout)

```python

from PyQt6.QtWidgets import QApplication,
QWidget, QVBoxLayout, QPushButton

app = QApplication([])
window = QWidget()
layout = QVBoxLayout()

layout.addWidget(QPushButton("Button 1"))
layout.addWidget(QPushButton("Button 2"))
layout.addWidget(QPushButton("Button 3"))

window.setLayout(layout)
window.show()
app.exec()
```

- The buttons **resize dynamically** when the window expands or shrinks.

Best for: Stacked layouts where components flow **vertically** or **horizontally**.

III. Making Kivy Layouts Responsive

Kivy supports **relative sizing** using percentages (`size_hint`).

Example: Responsive Kivy Layout

python

```
from kivy.app import App
from kivy.uix.button import Button
from kivy.uix.boxlayout import BoxLayout

class MyApp(App):
    def build(self):
        layout = BoxLayout()
        btn1    =    Button(text="Button    1",
size_hint=(0.5, 0.5))  # 50% of parent width &
height
        btn2    =    Button(text="Button    2",
size_hint=(0.5, 0.5))
        layout.add_widget(btn1)
        layout.add_widget(btn2)
        return layout

MyApp().run()
```

- `size_hint=(0.5, 0.5)` makes each button **scale dynamically**.

85

Best for: Mobile-friendly layouts and **scalable UI elements**.

IV. Making wxPython Layouts Flexible

wxPython provides `wx.BoxSizer` to handle layout resizing.

Example: wxPython Responsive Layout

```python
python

import wx

app = wx.App(False)
frame = wx.Frame(None, wx.ID_ANY, "wxPython Example")

panel = wx.Panel(frame)
sizer = wx.BoxSizer(wx.VERTICAL)

button1 = wx.Button(panel, label="Button 1")
button2 = wx.Button(panel, label="Button 2")

sizer.Add(button1, proportion=1, flag=wx.EXPAND | wx.ALL, border=5)
```

```
sizer.Add(button2, proportion=1, flag=wx.EXPAND
| wx.ALL, border=5)

panel.SetSizer(sizer)
frame.Show()
app.MainLoop()
```

- The `wx.EXPAND` flag ensures buttons resize dynamically.

Best for: Native-looking **desktop applications** with resizable components.

5.3 Summary: Key Takeaways for Responsive UI

Strategy	Best For	Example Frameworks
Grid Layouts	Dynamic UI scaling	PyQt, wxPython
Box Layouts	Auto-adjusting UI elements	PyQt, wxPython, Kivy
Size-Hinted Components	Proportional resizing	Kivy

Strategy	Best For	Example Frameworks
Native Look & Feel	OS-consistent UI	wxPython, PyQt
High-DPI Scaling	Sharp UI on 4K screens	PyQt, wxPython

Best Practices for Writing Adaptive Layouts:

1. **Use grid and box layouts** instead of absolute positioning.
2. **Avoid fixed-size elements** — use proportional (`size_hint`) or auto-sizing (`layout.addStretch()`).
3. **Test on different screen resolutions** using emulators or scaling settings.
4. **Use high-DPI scaling** (`Qt.HighDpiScaleFactorRoundingPolicy`) for modern displays.

Next Chapter Preview: Event-Driven Programming and Threading

In the next chapter, we will:

1. Explore **event-driven programming** to handle user interactions.

2. Learn **multithreading techniques** for keeping the UI responsive.

3. Implement **background processing** without freezing the interface.

Chapter 6

Event-Driven Programming and Threading

Modern desktop applications are **event-driven**, meaning they respond to user actions such as clicking a button, resizing a window, or typing in a text box. Additionally, running background tasks **without freezing the UI** is essential for a smooth user experience.

In this chapter, we will:

1. **Learn how event-driven programming works** and how to manage UI events.
2. **Implement threading and multiprocessing** to handle background tasks efficiently.

6.1 Managing UI Events and Background Tasks

I. Understanding Event-Driven Programming

1. Unlike procedural programs, which execute code **line by line**, **event-driven applications** wait for user actions (events) before executing code.
2. Common **events** include:
   - Clicking a button
   - Typing in a text field
   - Resizing a window
   - Selecting a menu item

Example: Simple Event Handling in PyQt

```python
python

from PyQt6.QtWidgets import QApplication,
QPushButton, QWidget, QVBoxLayout

def on_button_click():
    print("Button Clicked!")
```

```
app = QApplication([])
window = QWidget()
layout = QVBoxLayout()

button = QPushButton("Click Me")
button.clicked.connect(on_button_click)          #
Connect event to function

layout.addWidget(button)
window.setLayout(layout)
window.show()
app.exec()
```

- The **button click event** is connected to the on_button_click() function.
- When the user clicks the button, the function executes **without blocking the UI**.

Best for: Responding to user interactions in real time.

II. Using Event Loops to Handle Multiple Actions

Most GUI frameworks have an **event loop** that listens for user actions and updates the UI accordingly.

Example: Tkinter Event Loop

```python
python

import tkinter as tk

root = tk.Tk()

def on_key_press(event):
    print(f"Key Pressed: {event.char}")

root.bind("<KeyPress>", on_key_press)    # Listen
for keyboard events
root.mainloop()  # Start the event loop
```

- The **event loop** (`root.mainloop()`) continuously listens for user input.

Best for: Interactive applications that require real-time input handling.

6.2 Using Threading and Multiprocessing for Performance Optimization

I. Why Do We Need Threading?

1. **GUIs freeze** when performing long-running tasks (e.g., downloading a file).

2. Using **threads** allows background tasks to run **without blocking the UI**.

3. Python provides the `threading` and `multiprocessing` modules to handle concurrent tasks.

Example: Without Threading (Blocking the UI)

python

```python
import time
from PyQt6.QtWidgets import QApplication,
QPushButton, QWidget, QVBoxLayout

def long_task():
    time.sleep(5)  # Simulates a long process
    print("Task Completed!")

app = QApplication([])
window = QWidget()
layout = QVBoxLayout()

button = QPushButton("Start Task")
button.clicked.connect(long_task)  # UI Freezes!

layout.addWidget(button)
```

```
window.setLayout(layout)
window.show()
app.exec()
```

- Clicking the button **freezes the UI** for 5 seconds.
- **Solution:** Run `long_task()` in a separate thread.

II. Using Threads to Run Tasks in the Background

Example: Using `threading` to Prevent UI Freezing

```python

import time
import threading
from PyQt6.QtWidgets import QApplication,
QPushButton, QWidget, QVBoxLayout

def long_task():
    time.sleep(5)  # Simulates a long process
    print("Task Completed!")

def run_in_thread():
    thread = threading.Thread(target=long_task)
    thread.start()  # Run in background
```

95

```
app = QApplication([])
window = QWidget()
layout = QVBoxLayout()

button = QPushButton("Start Task")
button.clicked.connect(run_in_thread)   # Now UI
does not freeze

layout.addWidget(button)
window.setLayout(layout)
window.show()
app.exec()
```

- The **UI remains responsive** because `long_task()` runs in a separate thread.
- The **main event loop** continues running without being blocked.

Best for: Background tasks that **don't require UI updates**.

III. Updating the UI from a Background Thread

Threads **cannot directly modify the UI** in most frameworks (to avoid conflicts).

Solution: Use `QTimer.singleShot()` or `QMetaObject.invokeMethod()` in PyQt.

Example: Updating UI from a Thread (PyQt)

python

```
import time
import threading
from PyQt6.QtWidgets import QApplication,
QPushButton, QLabel, QWidget, QVBoxLayout

def long_task(label):
    time.sleep(5)
    label.setText("Task Completed!")  # UI update
from thread (causes error)

def run_in_thread(label):
    thread = threading.Thread(target=long_task,
args=(label,))
    thread.start()

app = QApplication([])
window = QWidget()
layout = QVBoxLayout()

label = QLabel("Click the button")
```

```
button = QPushButton("Start Task")
button.clicked.connect(lambda:
run_in_thread(label))  # Passing label

layout.addWidget(label)
layout.addWidget(button)
window.setLayout(layout)
window.show()
app.exec()
```

✖ **Problem:** Directly modifying the UI from another thread **may** **crash** **the** **app**. **Solution:** Use `QTimer.singleShot()` for safe UI updates.

IV. Using Multiprocessing for CPU-Intensive Tasks

The `threading` module does **not speed up CPU-bound tasks** due to Python's **Global Interpreter Lock (GIL)**. For CPU-intensive tasks (e.g., image processing, machine learning), use **multiprocessing** instead.

Example: Using `multiprocessing` for Heavy Computation

```
python

import multiprocessing

def compute_heavy_task(n):
    return sum(i * i for i in range(n))

if __name__ == "__main__":
    process                                    =
multiprocessing.Process(target=compute_heavy_ta
sk, args=(10000000,))
    process.start()
    process.join()
```

- **Threads** share memory but are limited by the GIL.
- **Processes** run independently, making them faster for heavy computations.

Best for: CPU-heavy tasks like **data processing, AI model training, and image rendering**.

6.3 Summary: Choosing Between Event Loops, Threads, and Multiprocessing

Method	Best For	Example Frameworks
Event Loops	Handling user inputs (clicks, keystrokes)	Tkinter, PyQt, wxPython
Threads (`threading`)	Background tasks (downloads, API calls)	PyQt, wxPython
Multiprocessing	CPU-intensive computations	General Python apps

Key Takeaways:

1. Use **event loops** for **handling UI actions** smoothly.

2. Use **threads** to run background tasks **without freezing the UI**.

3. Use **multiprocessing** for CPU-heavy tasks that require parallel execution.

4. Avoid **modifying the UI directly from a thread**—use framework-specific methods.

Next Chapter Preview: Deploying Cross-Platform Desktop Applications

In the next chapter, we will:

1. **Package Python applications** for Windows, macOS, and Linux.

2. Explore **PyInstaller, cx_Freeze, and PyOxidizer**.

3. Learn how to create **installers and executables** for easy distribution.

Chapter 7

Deploying Cross-Platform Desktop Applications

Once your desktop application is built, the next step is to package and distribute it across multiple operating systems. Unlike Python scripts (`.py` files), end-users expect standalone executables (`.exe` for Windows, `.app` for macOS, and ELF binaries for Linux).

In this chapter, we will:

1. **Learn how to package Python applications** using PyInstaller, cx_Freeze, and PyOxidizer.
2. **Distribute applications** on Windows, macOS, and Linux.

7.1 Packaging Python Applications for Different Platforms

Python applications need to be converted into **standalone executables** so that users can run them without installing Python or dependencies. Several tools exist for this:

Tool	Best For	Supported Platforms	Advantages
PyInstaller	General use, easy setup	Windows, macOS, Linux	Simple, widely used
cx_Freeze	Small apps, minimal dependencies	Windows, macOS, Linux	Lightweight output
PyOxidizer	Performance-optimized binaries	Windows, macOS, Linux	Faster startup, smaller size

I. Using PyInstaller for Cross-Platform Packaging

Installation:

```
sh
```

```
pip install pyinstaller
```

Basic Usage:

```
sh
```

```
pyinstaller --onefile my_script.py
```

- The `--onefile` flag **bundles everything into a single executable.**

Creating a GUI Application (Avoiding the Console Window)

```
sh
```

```
pyinstaller --onefile --windowed my_app.py
```

- The `--windowed` flag **hides the console** for GUI apps.

Specifying an Application Icon

```
sh
```

```
pyinstaller     --onefile     --windowed     --
icon=my_icon.ico my_app.py
```

Platform-Specific Notes:

- **Windows**: Produces an `.exe` file.
- **macOS**: Produces a `.app` bundle.
- **Linux**: Produces an ELF executable.

II. Using cx_Freeze for Lightweight Executables

Installation:

```sh
```

```sh
pip install cx_Freeze
```

Creating a `setup.py` File for cx_Freeze

```python
```

```python
from cx_Freeze import setup, Executable

setup(
    name="MyApp",
    version="1.0",
    description="A sample cross-platform app",
    executables=[Executable("my_app.py")]
```

)

Building the Executable:

sh

```
python setup.py build
```

- The output will be inside the `build/` folder.

III. Using PyOxidizer for Faster, Smaller Binaries

Installation:

sh

```
pip install pyoxidizer
```

Generating a Binary with PyOxidizer:

sh

```
pyoxidizer init-config
pyoxidizer build
```

- PyOxidizer embeds the Python interpreter inside the binary, making startup times **faster than PyInstaller or cx_Freeze**.

7.2 Distributing Applications on Windows, macOS, and Linux

I. Windows Distribution

Windows applications are typically distributed as:

1. **Standalone `.exe` Files** – Users download and run the executable.
2. **Installer Packages (`.msi` or `.exe`)** – Created using tools like `NSIS` or `Inno Setup`.

Creating a Windows Installer with Inno Setup

1. Install Inno Setup.
2. Write an `.iss` script:

```ini
[Setup]
AppName=MyApp
```

```
AppVersion=1.0
DefaultDirName={pf}\MyApp
OutputDir=.
OutputBaseFilename=MyAppInstaller
[Files]
Source:      "dist\my_app.exe";      DestDir:
"{app}"
[Icons]
Name:        "{app}\MyApp";        Filename:
"{app}\my_app.exe"
```

3. Compile the script to generate an installer.

Code-Signing for Windows Security Warnings
Windows may show a warning when running unsigned applications. To avoid this, purchase a **code-signing certificate** and sign the executable:

```sh
```

```
signtool        sign        /a        /t
http://timestamp.digicert.com my_app.exe
```

II. macOS Distribution

macOS applications are distributed as:

1. **App Bundles (`.app`)** – A self-contained macOS application package.
2. **Disk Images (`.dmg`)** – A mountable installer.

Creating a macOS `.app` Bundle

PyInstaller automatically creates a `.app` package:

sh

```
pyinstaller --onefile --windowed --icon=my_icon.icns my_app.py
```

Notarization for macOS Security Requirements

macOS requires apps to be **signed and notarized** to avoid security warnings.

sh

```
codesign --deep --force --verbose --sign "Developer ID Application: Your Name" my_app.app
xcrun altool --notarize-app --primary-bundle-id "com.yourcompany.myapp" --username "your_apple_id" --password "your_password" --file my_app.zip
```

III. Linux Distribution

Linux applications can be distributed as:

1. **Standalone Executables** – Created with PyInstaller or PyOxidizer.
2. **Debian Packages (`.deb`)** – Used for Ubuntu/Debian.
3. **RPM Packages (`.rpm`)** – Used for Fedora/CentOS.
4. **AppImages** – A portable application format for Linux.

Creating an AppImage for Linux

1. Install `linuxdeploy`:

```sh
wget
https://github.com/linuxdeploy/linuxdeplo
y/releases/latest/download/linuxdeploy-
x86_64.AppImage
chmod +x linuxdeploy-x86_64.AppImage
```

2. Bundle your app:

```sh
./linuxdeploy-x86_64.AppImage          --
appdir=AppDir --output appimage
```

Creating a `.deb` Package for Debian-Based Distros

1. Install `dpkg`:

```sh
sudo apt install dpkg-dev
```

2. Create a Debian package:

```sh
dpkg-deb --build my_app_folder my_app.deb
```

Flatpak & Snap for Universal Linux Distribution

- **Flatpak** (`flathub`) and **Snap** (`snapcraft`) allow universal packaging across Linux distributions.
- These formats provide **sandboxing** and **dependency management** for apps.

7.3 Summary: Choosing the Right Packaging and Distribution Method

Platform	Packaging Tool	Distribution Method
Windows	PyInstaller, cx_Freeze	`.exe`, `.msi`, Inno Setup

111

Platform	Packaging Tool	Distribution Method
macOS	PyInstaller, PyOxidizer	`.app`, `.dmg`, Notarization
Linux	PyInstaller, Snap	AppImage, `.deb`, `.rpm`, Flatpak

Key Takeaways:

1. **PyInstaller** is the easiest way to package Python apps across all platforms.

2. **cx_Freeze** is lightweight but requires more setup.

3. **PyOxidizer** creates **optimized, smaller binaries** with embedded Python.

4. **Windows apps require signing** to avoid security warnings.

5. **macOS apps require notarization** for smooth installation.

6. **Linux apps can be packaged as `.deb`, `.rpm`, or AppImages`.

Next Chapter Preview: Cross-Platform Testing Strategies

In the next chapter, we will:

1. Learn how to **test Python applications** on different operating systems.
2. Use **unit testing, UI testing, and automated testing tools**.
3. Set up **CI/CD pipelines for cross-platform testing**.

Chapter 7

Deploying Cross-Platform Desktop Applications

Deploying a Python desktop application involves converting the source code into an executable format that users can run without installing Python or dependencies. This process varies across operating systems, requiring different packaging tools and distribution methods.

In this chapter, we will:

1. Package Python applications using PyInstaller, cx_Freeze, and PyOxidizer.
2. Distribute applications on Windows, macOS, and Linux.

7.1 Packaging Python Applications for Different Platforms

Cross-platform applications must be packaged differently for each operating system. The three most commonly used tools for packaging Python applications are PyInstaller, cx_Freeze, and PyOxidizer.

I. PyInstaller

1. PyInstaller is a widely used tool for converting Python scripts into standalone executables.
2. It supports Windows, macOS, and Linux without requiring additional dependencies.
3. It bundles the Python interpreter, libraries, and scripts into a single executable file.

Installation:

sh

```
pip install pyinstaller
```

Creating an Executable:

sh

```
pyinstaller --onefile my_script.py
```

4. The `--onefile` flag creates a single executable file.
5. The `--windowed` flag prevents a terminal window from opening in GUI applications.

Example for GUI Applications:

sh

```
pyinstaller --onefile --windowed my_app.py
```

6. To specify an application icon, use the `--icon` flag:

sh

```
pyinstaller    --onefile    --windowed    --
icon=my_icon.ico my_app.py
```

II. cx_Freeze

1. cx_Freeze is a lightweight alternative to PyInstaller, best suited for simple applications with fewer dependencies.
2. It creates standalone executables but requires manual configuration.

Installation:

sh

```
pip install cx_Freeze
```

Creating a setup.py File:

python

```
from cx_Freeze import setup, Executable
```

```
setup(
    name="MyApp",
    version="1.0",
    description="A sample cross-platform app",
    executables=[Executable("my_app.py")]
)
```

Building the Executable:

```
sh
```

```
python setup.py build
```

III. PyOxidizer

1. PyOxidizer is an advanced tool that embeds Python within the executable for faster startup times and smaller file sizes.
2. It produces fully standalone binaries with no external dependencies.

Installation:

```
sh
```

```
pip install pyoxidizer
```

Building the Application:

```sh
pyoxidizer init-config
pyoxidizer build
```

7.2 Distributing Applications on Windows, macOS, and Linux

Each operating system has a preferred method for distributing applications.

I. Windows Distribution

1. Windows applications can be distributed as standalone `.exe` files or installer packages (`.msi`, `.exe`).
2. The most commonly used installer creation tools are Inno Setup and NSIS.

Creating an Installer with Inno Setup:

1. Install Inno Setup.
2. Write an `.iss` script:

```ini
[Setup]
AppName=MyApp
```

```
AppVersion=1.0
DefaultDirName={pf}\MyApp
OutputDir=.
OutputBaseFilename=MyAppInstaller
[Files]
Source: "dist\my_app.exe"; DestDir: "{app}"
[Icons]
Name:          "{app}\MyApp";          Filename:
"{app}\my_app.exe"
```

3.   Compile the script to generate an installer.

Code-Signing   for   Windows   Applications:
Windows may block unsigned applications. To avoid
security warnings, sign the executable:

```
sh
```

```
signtool          sign          /a          /t
http://timestamp.digicert.com my_app.exe
```

II. macOS Distribution

1.   macOS applications are typically distributed as `.app`
     bundles or `.dmg` disk images.
2.   Apple requires applications to be signed and notarized
     before distribution.

Creating a macOS `.app` Bundle:

sh

```
pyinstaller    --onefile    --windowed    --
icon=my_icon.icns my_app.py
```

Notarizing a macOS Application:

sh

```
codesign   --deep   --force   --verbose   --sign
"Developer ID Application: Your Name" my_app.app
xcrun altool --notarize-app --primary-bundle-id
"com.yourcompany.myapp"              --username
"your_apple_id"  --password "your_password"  --
file my_app.zip
```

III. Linux Distribution

1. Linux applications can be distributed as standalone executables, `.deb` packages, `.rpm` packages, or AppImages.
2. AppImages are the easiest way to distribute Linux applications since they do not require installation.

Creating an AppImage for Linux:

120

1. Install `linuxdeploy`:

sh

```
wget
https://github.com/linuxdeploy/linuxdeploy/rele
ases/latest/download/linuxdeploy-
x86_64.AppImage
chmod +x linuxdeploy-x86_64.AppImage
```

2. Bundle the application:

sh

```
./linuxdeploy-x86_64.AppImage --appdir=AppDir --
output appimage
```

Creating a `.deb` Package for Debian-Based Distributions:

sh

```
dpkg-deb --build my_app_folder my_app.deb
```

Flatpak and Snap for Universal Linux Distribution:

1. Flatpak and Snap allow universal packaging across multiple Linux distributions.

2. These formats ensure proper dependency management and sandboxing for applications.

7.3 Summary: Choosing the Right Packaging and Distribution Method

1. PyInstaller is the easiest tool for packaging Python applications across all platforms.

2. cx_Freeze produces lightweight executables but requires additional setup.

3. PyOxidizer creates optimized binaries with embedded Python, improving performance.

4. Windows applications require signing to avoid security warnings.

5. macOS applications require notarization to comply with Apple's security requirements.

6. Linux applications can be packaged as `.deb`, `.rpm`, or AppImages for easier distribution.

Next Chapter Preview: Cross-Platform Testing Strategies

1. Learn how to test Python applications on different operating systems.

2. Use unit testing, UI testing, and automated testing tools.

3. Set up CI/CD pipelines for cross-platform testing.

Part 3

Developing Web-Based Applications with Python

Chapter 8

Python for the Web: Backend and Frontend Integration

Python is widely used for web development, offering powerful frameworks like Flask, Django, and FastAPI for building backend services. Unlike desktop applications, web applications run in a browser and interact with servers, enabling cross-platform accessibility.

In this chapter, we will:

1. Explore Flask, Django, and FastAPI for developing cross-platform web applications.
2. Understand how web applications differ from native desktop applications.

8.1 Flask, Django, and FastAPI for Cross-Platform Web Applications

Python provides multiple web frameworks suited for different use cases. Flask, Django, and FastAPI are among the most popular options, each offering unique advantages.

I. Flask: Lightweight and Flexible Web Framework

1. Flask is a micro-framework that provides essential web functionalities without enforcing a strict project structure.
2. It is best suited for small to medium-sized applications that require customization.
3. Flask follows a minimalistic approach, allowing developers to choose components as needed.

Installation:

```sh
pip install flask
```

Basic Flask Application:

```python
from flask import Flask

app = Flask(__name__)

@app.route("/")
def home():
```

126

```
    return "Hello, Flask!"

if __name__ == "__main__":
    app.run(debug=True)
```

4. Flask provides built-in routing, request handling, and session management.

5. It supports RESTful APIs and integrates easily with frontend frameworks like React and Vue.js.

II. Django: Full-Stack Web Framework

1. Django is a high-level web framework that includes built-in functionalities for authentication, database management, and security.

2. It follows the **Model-View-Template (MVT)** architecture, promoting modular development.

3. Django is best suited for large-scale applications requiring rapid development and scalability.

Installation:

```sh
sh

pip install django
```

127

Creating a Django Project:

```sh
```

```sh
django-admin startproject myproject
cd myproject
python manage.py runserver
```

1. Django includes a built-in ORM (Object-Relational Mapper) for database interactions.
2. It offers built-in admin panels for managing content and users.

III. FastAPI: High-Performance Web Framework for APIs

1. FastAPI is designed for building high-performance APIs with automatic documentation.
2. It is asynchronous, making it significantly faster than Flask and Django for handling multiple requests.
3. FastAPI is best suited for microservices and applications requiring real-time communication.

Installation:

```sh
```

```
pip install fastapi uvicorn
```

Basic FastAPI Application:

```python
python

from fastapi import FastAPI

app = FastAPI()

@app.get("/")
def read_root():
    return {"message": "Hello, FastAPI!"}

if __name__ == "__main__":
    import uvicorn
    uvicorn.run(app,             host="127.0.0.1",
port=8000)
```

4. FastAPI supports automatic validation using Python type hints.

5. It generates OpenAPI documentation for API endpoints automatically.

IV. Comparison of Flask, Django, and FastAPI

Feature	Flask	Django	FastAPI
Best For	Small to medium apps	Large, scalable apps	APIs and microservices
Performance	Moderate	Moderate	High (async)
Ease of Use	Easy	Moderate	Easy
Built-in Features	Minimal	Full-stack	API-focused
Database Support	External ORM needed	Built-in ORM	External ORM needed

8.2 How Web Applications Differ from Native Desktop Applications

Web applications and desktop applications serve different purposes and have distinct architectures.

I. Deployment and Accessibility

1. **Web applications** run on a server and are accessed through a web browser.

2. **Desktop applications** run locally on a user's operating system.

3. Web applications allow cross-platform access without requiring installation.

II. User Interface and Experience

1. Web applications use **HTML, CSS, and JavaScript** for frontend rendering.

2. Desktop applications rely on native GUI frameworks such as **PyQt, Tkinter, or wxPython**.

3. Web applications require an internet connection, while desktop applications can function offline.

III. Performance and Resource Usage

1. **Desktop applications** can access system resources (GPU, filesystem) directly.

2. **Web applications** are sandboxed and have limited access to the system.

3. Web applications rely on **client-server architecture**, where processing is distributed between the browser and the backend.

IV. Security Considerations

1. Web applications are exposed to security threats like **SQL injection, XSS (Cross-Site Scripting), and CSRF (Cross-Site Request Forgery)**.

2. Desktop applications may have vulnerabilities related to **file access, local privilege escalation, and malware injection**.

3. Web applications require **HTTPS, authentication mechanisms, and API security** for protection.

V. Development and Maintenance

1. Web applications require separate development for **frontend (React, Vue.js, Angular)** and **backend (Flask, Django, FastAPI)**.

2. Desktop applications integrate frontend and backend logic within the same application.

3. Web applications allow **continuous deployment and updates**, whereas desktop applications require users to install updates manually.

8.3 Summary

1. Flask, Django, and FastAPI are powerful frameworks for building Python-based web applications.

2. Flask is best for small applications, Django is suited for large-scale projects, and FastAPI is optimized for API development.

3. Web applications differ from desktop applications in terms of accessibility, UI, performance, security, and maintenance.

4. Web applications use a **client-server model**, whereas desktop applications run locally.

5. Security concerns in web applications require **proper authentication, HTTPS encryption, and API security measures**.

Next Chapter Preview: Building Cross-Platform APIs and Microservices

1. Learn how to create RESTful APIs with Flask, Django, and FastAPI.

2. Implement authentication and authorization for secure APIs.

3. Optimize APIs for performance, scalability, and cross-platform accessibility.

Chapter 9

Building Cross-Platform APIs and Microservices

APIs (Application Programming Interfaces) enable communication between different software systems, making them essential for cross-platform development. Python provides powerful frameworks to build APIs that work across devices, operating systems, and cloud platforms.

In this chapter, we will:

1. Learn how to design RESTful and GraphQL APIs.
2. Explore cloud hosting options for universal accessibility.

9.1 Designing RESTful and GraphQL APIs

APIs are broadly categorized into two types: RESTful APIs and GraphQL APIs.

I. RESTful API Design

1. REST (Representational State Transfer) is a widely used architectural style for web APIs.

2. It relies on standard HTTP methods such as **GET, POST, PUT, DELETE**.

3. RESTful APIs follow **resource-based URL patterns**.

Example REST API Endpoints:

- `GET /users` → Retrieve all users.
- `GET /users/{id}` → Retrieve a specific user.
- `POST /users` → Create a new user.
- `PUT /users/{id}` → Update a user.
- `DELETE /users/{id}` → Delete a user.

Building a REST API with Flask:

```python
from flask import Flask, jsonify, request

app = Flask(__name__)

users = [{"id": 1, "name": "Alice"}, {"id": 2,
"name": "Bob"}]

@app.route("/users", methods=["GET"])
def get_users():
    return jsonify(users)
```

```
@app.route("/users/<int:user_id>",
methods=["GET"])
def get_user(user_id):
    user = next((u for u in users if u["id"] ==
user_id), None)
    return jsonify(user) if user else ("User not
found", 404)

if __name__ == "__main__":
    app.run(debug=True)
```

4. Flask is a lightweight framework that allows rapid API development.
5. REST APIs return **JSON responses**, making them easy to integrate with web and mobile applications.

II. GraphQL API Design

1. GraphQL is an alternative to REST that allows clients to request only the data they need.
2. It eliminates **over-fetching and under-fetching** of data.
3. Instead of multiple endpoints, GraphQL uses a **single endpoint (/graphql)** for all requests.

Installing GraphQL for Python:

```
sh
```

```
pip install graphene
```

Building a GraphQL API with Flask:

```python
python

from flask import Flask
from flask_graphql import GraphQLView
import graphene

class User(graphene.ObjectType):
    id = graphene.Int()
    name = graphene.String()

class Query(graphene.ObjectType):
    users = graphene.List(User)

    def resolve_users(self, info):
        return [{"id": 1, "name": "Alice"},
{"id": 2, "name": "Bob"}]

schema = graphene.Schema(query=Query)

app = Flask(__name__)
app.add_url_rule("/graphql",
view_func=GraphQLView.as_view("graphql",
schema=schema, graphiql=True))

if __name__ == "__main__":
```

```
app.run(debug=True)
```

1. GraphQL enables **precise data fetching**, reducing network overhead.
2. It is beneficial for applications requiring **complex queries and nested data**.

III. REST vs. GraphQL: When to Use Which?

1. **Use REST if:**
   1. The API structure is simple and follows a resource-based model.
   2. The application requires standard CRUD operations.
   3. The API needs to be easily cacheable.
2. **Use GraphQL if:**
   1. The API requires **dynamic queries** instead of fixed responses.
   2. The frontend needs control over **which fields to fetch**.
   3. The application retrieves deeply nested data frequently.

9.2 Hosting on Cloud Services for Universal Accessibility

After developing an API, hosting it on a cloud platform ensures accessibility from anywhere.

I. Cloud Hosting Options

1. **AWS Lambda with API Gateway**
   - Serverless deployment, automatically scales with traffic.
   - Ideal for microservices that require cost-effective scaling.

2. **Google Cloud Run**
   - Runs containerized Python APIs with automatic scaling.
   - Supports Flask, FastAPI, and Django applications.

3. **Heroku**
   - Easy-to-use platform for deploying Python web apps and APIs.
   - Supports **Flask and Django** out of the box.

4. **Azure App Service**
   - Deploys Flask, Django, and FastAPI applications with minimal configuration.

o   Offers built-in scaling and monitoring.

II. Deploying a Flask API on Heroku

1. Install the Heroku CLI:

```sh
curl                          https://cli-
assets.heroku.com/install.sh | sh
```

2. Create a `requirements.txt` file:

```sh
flask
gunicorn
```

3. Create a `Procfile` for Heroku deployment:

```sh
web: gunicorn app:app
```

4. Deploy the application:

```sh
heroku login
```

```
heroku create my-python-api
git init
git add .
git commit -m "Deploy API"
git push heroku main
```

III. Deploying a FastAPI App on AWS Lambda

1. Install dependencies:

```sh
```

```
pip install fastapi mangum
```

2. Create an `app.py` file:

```python
```

```
from fastapi import FastAPI
from mangum import Mangum

app = FastAPI()

@app.get("/")
def home():
    return {"message": "Deployed on AWS Lambda"}
```

```
handler = Mangum(app)
```

3. Deploy using AWS Lambda with API Gateway.

IV. Scaling APIs with Docker and Kubernetes

1. **Docker** allows APIs to run in isolated environments.
2. **Kubernetes** automates deployment, scaling, and management of API containers.
3. APIs can be deployed in **multi-node clusters** for high availability.

Creating a Dockerfile for a Flask API:

```dockerfile
dockerfile

FROM python:3.9
WORKDIR /app
COPY . /app
RUN pip install -r requirements.txt
CMD ["gunicorn", "app:app"]
```

Running the Flask API in a Docker container:

```sh
sh
```

```
docker build -t my-api .
docker run -p 5000:5000 my-api
```

9.3 Summary

1. RESTful APIs use standard HTTP methods, while GraphQL APIs allow dynamic data queries.
2. Flask is best for lightweight APIs, Django is suitable for full-stack web apps, and FastAPI is optimized for high-performance APIs.
3. Cloud hosting ensures APIs are accessible from anywhere.
4. AWS Lambda, Google Cloud Run, and Heroku provide easy deployment options.
5. Docker and Kubernetes enable **scalability and containerized API deployment**.

Next Chapter Preview: Creating Progressive Web Applications (PWAs) with Python

1. Learn how to build web applications that behave like native apps.
2. Implement offline capabilities and push notifications.

3. Optimize performance using service workers and caching techniques.

Chapter 10

Creating Progressive Web Applications (PWAs) with Python

Progressive Web Applications (PWAs) bridge the gap between traditional web applications and native desktop or mobile apps. They offer a fast, reliable, and engaging user experience, enabling web applications to behave like native apps by supporting offline usage, push notifications, and background synchronization.

In this chapter, we will:

1. Explore how to make web applications feel like native desktop or mobile apps.
2. Implement offline capabilities and push notifications in a Python-based PWA.

10.1 Making Web Apps Feel Like Native Desktop or Mobile Apps

PWAs leverage modern web technologies to deliver an app-like experience in a browser. The key features that make a PWA feel like a native app include:

I. Characteristics of PWAs

1. **Installable** – Users can install a PWA on their home screen like a regular app.
2. **Offline Support** – The application works even when the user is offline.
3. **Responsive** – The UI adapts to different screen sizes and resolutions.
4. **Background Sync** – Data synchronization continues even when the app is in the background.
5. **Push Notifications** – Users receive notifications even when the app is not open.

II. Converting a Flask Web App into a PWA

A Flask-based web application can be enhanced into a PWA by adding:

1. A **Web App Manifest** to define the app's metadata.
2. A **Service Worker** to handle caching and offline functionality.

1. Creating a Web App Manifest (`manifest.json`)

1. The manifest file describes the app's appearance when installed.
2. It specifies the app's name, icons, and start URL.

json

```json
{
    "name": "My PWA",
    "short_name": "PWA",
    "start_url": "/",
    "display": "standalone",
    "background_color": "#ffffff",
    "theme_color": "#000000",
    "icons": [
        {
            "src": "/static/icon-192x192.png",
            "sizes": "192x192",
            "type": "image/png"
        },
```

```
{
    "src": "/static/icon-512x512.png",
    "sizes": "512x512",
    "type": "image/png"
  }
 ]
}
```

3. The `"display"`: `"standalone"` option ensures the PWA runs as an independent app.

4. The `"start_url"`: `"/"` loads the app's homepage when launched.

2. Registering a Service Worker (`service-worker.js`)

1. A **service worker** enables offline functionality by caching resources.

2. It intercepts network requests and serves cached files when offline.

```js
self.addEventListener("install", (event) => {
  event.waitUntil(
    caches.open("pwa-cache").then((cache) => {
      return                    cache.addAll(["/",
"/static/style.css",              "/static/icon-
192x192.png"]);
    })
```

```
  );
});

self.addEventListener("fetch", (event) => {
  event.respondWith(
    caches.match(event.request).then((response)
=> {
      return response || fetch(event.request);
    })
  );
});
```

3. The install event caches essential assets for offline use.

4. The fetch event serves cached files when the network is unavailable.

3. Registering the Service Worker in Flask (index.html)

html

```
<script>
  if ("serviceWorker" in navigator) {

navigator.serviceWorker.register("/static/servi
ce-worker.js").then(() => {
      console.log("Service Worker Registered");
    });
  }
</script>
```

5. The service worker is registered when the page loads, enabling offline functionality.

III. Installing the PWA on a Device

1. The PWA can be installed when accessed through a browser like Chrome, Edge, or Safari.
2. The browser will prompt the user to "Add to Home Screen" if the PWA meets installation criteria.

10.2 Offline Capabilities and Push Notifications

Offline capabilities allow PWAs to function even without an internet connection. Push notifications enhance user engagement by sending updates in real time.

I. Implementing Offline Mode in a Python PWA

1. The **service worker** caches resources, enabling offline access.
2. IndexedDB can be used to store data locally for later synchronization.

Using Flask to Handle Data Storage for Offline Mode:

python

```python
from flask import Flask, request, jsonify

app = Flask(__name__)

@app.route("/sync", methods=["POST"])
def sync_data():
    data = request.json
    print("Received offline data:", data)
    return jsonify({"status": "success"}), 200

if __name__ == "__main__":
    app.run(debug=True)
```

3. When the internet is restored, the app sends the locally stored data to the server for synchronization.

Using JavaScript to Sync Data When Online:

js

```js
window.addEventListener("online", () => {
  let              offlineData              =
localStorage.getItem("offline_data");
  if (offlineData) {
    fetch("/sync", {
```

```
    method: "POST",
    body: offlineData,
    headers:            {           "Content-Type":
"application/json" }
    }).then(()                                      =>
localStorage.removeItem("offline_data"));
  }
});
```

II. Implementing Push Notifications

1. Push notifications require **Firebase Cloud Messaging (FCM)** or **Web Push API**.
2. The server sends a message to the client when an event occurs.

1. Installing the pywebpush *Library*
sh

```
pip install pywebpush
```

2. Sending Push Notifications from Flask
python

```
from pywebpush import webpush

def    send_push_notification(subscription_info,
message):
    webpush(
```

```
        subscription_info=subscription_info,
        data=message,
        vapid_private_key="your-private-key",
        vapid_claims={"sub":        "mailto:your-
email@example.com"}
    )
```

3. The server sends a notification when a new event occurs.

4. The user receives a notification even if the PWA is not open.

III. Handling Push Notifications in the Service Worker

```
js
```

```js
self.addEventListener("push", (event) => {
   const options = { body: event.data.text(),
icon: "/static/icon-192x192.png" };

event.waitUntil(self.registration.showNotificat
ion("New Update", options));
});
```

5. When the server sends a push notification, the service worker displays a message.

IV. Benefits of Push Notifications in PWAs

1. **Real-time updates** keep users engaged.
2. Notifications can **increase user retention** and app usage.
3. **Works even when the app is closed**, improving accessibility.

10.3 Summary

1. PWAs combine the best features of web and native apps, providing an installable and offline-capable experience.
2. A **web app manifest** defines how a PWA appears and behaves when installed.
3. A **service worker** enables caching, offline mode, and background tasks.
4. IndexedDB or local storage allows **offline data persistence and synchronization**.
5. Push notifications increase user engagement by delivering real-time updates.

Next Chapter Preview: Optimizing Web Applications for Performance

1. Learn how to reduce load times with caching, compression, and lazy loading.
2. Optimize Python web applications using asynchronous processing.
3. Implement performance monitoring and debugging techniques.

Chapter 11

Introduction to Mobile Development with Python

Python is widely used in web and desktop development, but it is also gaining traction in mobile application development. While native mobile applications are typically developed using Java/Kotlin for Android and Swift/Objective-C for iOS, Python frameworks like **Kivy, BeeWare, and PyQt** provide cross-platform solutions for building mobile applications.

In this chapter, we will:

1. Compare Kivy, BeeWare, and PyQt for mobile app development.
2. Explore the challenges of mobile development with Python and their solutions.

11.1 Comparing Kivy, BeeWare, and PyQt for Mobile Apps

Python offers multiple frameworks for mobile development. Each has unique strengths and is suited for different use cases.

I. Kivy: Open-Source Framework for Multi-Touch Apps

1. **Kivy** is an open-source Python library designed for rapid development of multitouch applications.
2. It supports Android, iOS, Windows, macOS, and Linux.
3. Kivy uses a unique design language (KV) for UI development.

Installation:

```sh
```

```sh
pip install kivy
```

Example Kivy App:

```python
```

```
from kivy.app import App
from kivy.uix.button import Button

class MyApp(App):
    def build(self):
        return Button(text="Hello, Kivy!")

MyApp().run()
```

4. **Advantages of Kivy:**
   o Works across multiple platforms.
   o Supports multi-touch gestures.
   o GPU-accelerated rendering.

5. **Disadvantages of Kivy:**
   o UI does not have a native look.
   o Performance optimization is required for complex apps.

II. BeeWare: Native Look and Feel for Mobile Apps

1. **BeeWare** allows developers to write Python applications that run natively on Android, iOS, Windows, macOS, and Linux.

2. It uses **Toga**, a native GUI toolkit for building platform-specific UIs.

3. BeeWare converts Python code into native binaries for mobile devices.

Installation:

sh

```
pip install briefcase
```

Creating a BeeWare App:

sh

```
briefcase new
briefcase dev
```

4. **Advantages of BeeWare:**
   o Produces truly native applications.
   o Uses platform-specific UI components.
   o Supports Python 3 with minimal modifications.

5. **Disadvantages of BeeWare:**
   o Still under active development, so documentation may be limited.
   o Requires platform-specific build configurations.

III. PyQt: Feature-Rich but Less Mobile-Friendly

1. **PyQt** is a powerful framework primarily used for desktop applications, but it also supports Android and iOS with some modifications.
2. It provides a rich set of UI components but lacks dedicated mobile support.

Installation:

```sh
sh
```

```sh
pip install PyQt6
```

Example PyQt App:

```python
python
```

```python
from PyQt6.QtWidgets import QApplication, QPushButton, QWidget

app = QApplication([])
window = QWidget()
button = QPushButton("Hello, PyQt!", parent=window)
```

```
window.show()
app.exec()
```

3. **Advantages of PyQt:**
   o Provides extensive UI components.
   o Great for cross-platform desktop applications.

4. **Disadvantages of PyQt:**
   o Not optimized for mobile app development.
   o Lacks built-in touch support.

IV. Comparison of Kivy, BeeWare, and PyQt for Mobile Development

Feature	Kivy	BeeWare	PyQt
Best For	Multi-touch & graphical apps	Native-looking apps	Desktop applications
Platform Support	Android, iOS, Windows, macOS, Linux	Android, iOS, Windows, macOS, Linux	Limited mobile support
Performance	Moderate	High	High (but not optimized for mobile)

Feature	Kivy	BeeWare	PyQt
Ease of Development	Moderate	Moderate	Hard
Native UI Look	No	Yes	Partial

11.2 Challenges and Solutions for Mobile Development with Python

Python-based mobile development comes with several challenges that developers must address.

I. Challenge: Performance Limitations

1. Python is **interpreted**, making it slower than compiled languages like Swift and Kotlin.
2. Heavy computational tasks may cause performance issues.

Solution:

1. Use **Cython** to compile Python into C for performance gains.

2. Optimize Python code using **NumPy and multiprocessing** for intensive calculations.

II. Challenge: Limited Access to Native Mobile APIs

1. Mobile applications require access to APIs like camera, GPS, and notifications.
2. Python frameworks do not provide direct access to these APIs.

Solution:

1. Use **Pyjnius** (for Kivy) to interact with Android APIs.
2. Use **Rubicon ObjC** (for BeeWare) to access iOS APIs.

Example: Using Pyjnius to Access Android APIs in Kivy:

python

```
from jnius import autoclass

MediaPlayer                                =
autoclass("android.media.MediaPlayer")
player = MediaPlayer()
player.setDataSource("/path/to/audio.mp3")
player.prepare()
```

```
player.start()
```

III. Challenge: Packaging and Distribution

1. Packaging Python apps for iOS and Android is **not straightforward**.
2. Google Play and Apple App Store require **native executables**.

Solution:

1. Use **Buildozer** for packaging Kivy apps into `.apk` for Android.
2. Use **Briefcase** for creating iOS `.app` bundles with BeeWare.

Building an Android App with Buildozer:

```sh
pip install buildozer
buildozer init
buildozer -v android debug
```

IV. Challenge: UI Design and User Experience

1. Kivy applications do not have a **native look and feel**.
2. Users expect apps to match **OS-specific UI guidelines**.

Solution:

1. Use **BeeWare** if a native UI is required.
2. Customize Kivy themes to resemble mobile OS designs.

Example: Styling a Kivy App with a Custom Theme:

python

```
from kivy.lang import Builder

KV = """
BoxLayout:
    Button:
        text: "Hello, Kivy!"
        background_color: 0.2, 0.6, 0.8, 1
"""

from kivy.app import App

class MyApp(App):
    def build(self):
```

```
return Builder.load_string(KV)

MyApp().run()
```

V. Challenge: App Store Approval

1. Python apps may be rejected due to **non-native components**.
2. App store policies require **code signing and performance optimization**.

Solution:

1. Follow **Google Play and Apple App Store** guidelines for submission.
2. Ensure apps are **signed and optimized** before deployment.

11.3 Summary

1. **Kivy** is best for touch-based, graphical applications with multi-platform support.
2. **BeeWare** creates **truly native** apps with platform-specific UI elements.
3. **PyQt** is more suited for desktop applications, with limited mobile support.

4. Performance limitations can be mitigated using **Cython and optimized Python libraries**.

5. Packaging and distribution challenges can be addressed using **Buildozer (for Android) and Briefcase (for iOS)**.

6. To meet app store requirements, ensure **proper UI design, performance optimization, and native API integration**.

Next Chapter Preview: Building Native-Like Apps with Kivy and BeeWare

1. Learn how to create a complete mobile application using **Kivy and BeeWare**.

2. Implement platform-specific features such as **touch gestures, animations, and notifications**.

3. Deploy mobile apps to **Google Play Store and Apple App Store**.

Chapter 12

Building Native-Like Apps with Kivy and BeeWare

Developing mobile applications with Python requires frameworks that support cross-platform deployment while maintaining a native user experience. **Kivy** and **BeeWare** are two of the most popular frameworks for Python mobile development.

In this chapter, we will:

1. Build a simple cross-platform mobile application using **Kivy and BeeWare**.
2. Explore UI components and mobile-specific considerations to enhance usability.

12.1 Hands-On Development: Creating a Simple Cross-Platform Mobile App

To demonstrate the capabilities of both **Kivy and BeeWare**, we will build a basic "To-Do List" application that works on **Android, iOS, Windows, macOS, and Linux**.

I. Setting Up Kivy for Mobile Development

1. Install **Kivy**:

   sh

   ```
   pip install kivy
   ```

2. Install **Buildozer** (for Android deployment):

   sh

   ```
   pip install buildozer
   ```

3. Install **Pyjnius** for Android API access:

   sh

   ```
   pip install pyjnius
   ```

II. Creating a Simple To-Do App with Kivy

1. Create a new Python file (todo_kivy.py):

   python

```
from kivy.app import App
from kivy.uix.boxlayout import BoxLayout
from kivy.uix.textinput import TextInput
from kivy.uix.button import Button
from kivy.uix.label import Label

class ToDoApp(App):
    def build(self):
        self.layout                 =
BoxLayout(orientation="vertical")
        self.task_input             =
TextInput(hint_text="Enter task")
        self.add_button = Button(text="Add
Task")
        self.task_list              =
BoxLayout(orientation="vertical")


self.add_button.bind(on_press=self.add_ta
sk)


self.layout.add_widget(self.task_input)

self.layout.add_widget(self.add_button)

self.layout.add_widget(self.task_list)
```

```
        return self.layout

    def add_task(self, instance):
        task_text = self.task_input.text
        if task_text:
            task_label                    =
Label(text=task_text,    size_hint_y=None,
height=40)

        self.task_list.add_widget(task_label)
            self.task_input.text = ""

if __name__ == "__main__":
    ToDoApp().run()
```

2. **Understanding the UI components used in Kivy**:

- o   BoxLayout arranges widgets vertically.
- o   TextInput allows user input.
- o   Button triggers an event when clicked.
- o   Label displays the entered tasks.

3. **Running the application on Android**:

```sh
sh
```

```
buildozer -v android debug
```

III. Setting Up BeeWare for Mobile Development

1. Install **BeeWare**:

   sh

   ```
   pip install briefcase
   ```

2. Create a new **BeeWare project**:

   sh

   ```
   briefcase new
   cd myproject
   briefcase dev
   ```

IV. Creating a Simple To-Do App with BeeWare

1. Modify `app.py` to implement the UI:

   python

   ```
   from toga import App, Box, Button,
   TextInput, Label, ScrollContainer
   ```

```
class ToDoApp(App):
    def startup(self):
        self.main_box = Box()
        self.task_input                    =
TextInput(placeholder="Enter task")
        self.add_button    =    Button("Add
Task", on_press=self.add_task)
        self.task_list = Box()
        self.scroll_container              =
ScrollContainer(content=self.task_list)


self.main_box.add(self.task_input)


self.main_box.add(self.add_button)


self.main_box.add(self.scroll_container)


        self.main_window                   =
self.main_window
        self.main_window.content           =
self.main_box
        self.main_window.show()

    def add_task(self, widget):
        task_text = self.task_input.value
        if task_text:
            task_label = Label(task_text)
```

173

```
self.task_list.add(task_label)
        self.task_input.value = ""

def main():
    return        ToDoApp("To-Do        App",
"com.example.todo")

if __name__ == "__main__":
    main().main_loop()
```

2. **Running the BeeWare application on Android**:

```sh
sh

briefcase build android
briefcase run android
```

V. Comparison of Kivy and BeeWare Implementation

Feature	Kivy	BeeWare
UI Rendering	Uses OpenGL for rendering	Uses native UI elements

Feature	Kivy	BeeWare
Ease of Use	Requires learning Kivy language	Follows standard Python OOP principles
Performance	Good for graphical apps	Faster for native UI apps
Platform Support	Android, Desktop	iOS, Android, iOS, Windows, macOS, Linux

12.2 UI Components and Mobile-Specific Considerations

When designing mobile applications, the UI must be responsive, touch-friendly, and optimized for small screens.

I. Mobile UI Components in Kivy and BeeWare

1. **TextInput** – Allows users to enter text.
2. **Buttons** – Provide interactive controls for user actions.
3. **Labels** – Display static text.
4. **Scroll Containers** – Enable scrolling when content overflows.

5. **Dialogs & Alerts** – Provide notifications and confirmations.

II. Optimizing UI for Mobile Screens

1. **Use Auto-Sizing Layouts** – Avoid fixed sizes, use percentage-based layouts.
2. **Ensure Touch-Friendly Buttons** – Use larger buttons for better usability.
3. **Support Different Screen Sizes** – Test on multiple devices.
4. **Minimize Background Processes** – Avoid running heavy tasks in the main thread.

III. Mobile Performance Considerations

1. **Reduce Memory Usage** – Avoid storing large data in memory.
2. **Use Asynchronous Processing** – Run background tasks using `asyncio` or `threading`.
3. **Enable Hardware Acceleration** – Use GPU rendering where available.

12.3 Summary

1. Kivy is well-suited for custom UI designs and multi-touch applications.
2. BeeWare provides a **native look and feel** for mobile applications.
3. The **To-Do List** app demonstrated how to implement UI components in both frameworks.
4. UI considerations such as **auto-sizing, touch-friendly design, and scroll support** are essential for mobile apps.
5. Performance optimization techniques such as **asynchronous processing and GPU acceleration** enhance the user experience.

Next Chapter Preview: Deploying Mobile Applications on iOS and Android

1. Learn how to package Python mobile apps for distribution.
2. Sign and upload applications to the Google Play Store and Apple App Store.
3. Implement security measures and app store compliance.

Chapter 13

Deploying Mobile Applications on iOS and Android

Once a mobile application is developed using **Kivy or BeeWare**, the next step is to package and distribute it for **Android (Google Play Store) and iOS (Apple App Store)**. Python-based apps require specific tools to convert the code into native executables.

In this chapter, we will:

1. Learn how to package Python mobile applications using **Buildozer (for Kivy) and Briefcase (for BeeWare)**.
2. Explore the steps required to **publish apps on the Google Play Store and Apple App Store**.

13.1 Packaging with Buildozer and Briefcase

I. Using Buildozer to Package Kivy Apps for Android

Buildozer automates the process of converting a Kivy application into an `.apk` (Android Package).

1. Setting Up Buildozer

1. Install Buildozer and dependencies:

    sh

    ```
    pip install buildozer
    sudo apt update && sudo apt install -y
    python3-pip git zip unzip openjdk-11-jdk
    ```

2. Navigate to the Kivy project directory and initialize Buildozer:

    sh

    ```
    buildozer init
    ```

3. This generates a `buildozer.spec` configuration file.

2. Configuring buildozer.spec for Android

1. Open `buildozer.spec` and modify key settings:

    ini

    ```
    package.name = MyKivyApp
    ```

179

```
package.domain = com.example
package.version = 1.0
android.p4a_dir = ./p4a
android.permissions     =     INTERNET,
WRITE_EXTERNAL_STORAGE
```

2. Ensure `android.ndk` and `android.api` versions are set correctly.

3. Building the APK File

1. Run the following command to package the app:

sh

```
buildozer -v android debug
```

2. The `.apk` file will be generated in the `bin/` directory.
3. To test the application on an Android device, connect via USB and install the APK:

sh

```
adb install bin/mykivyapp-1.0-arm64-v8a-
debug.apk
```

II. Using Briefcase to Package BeeWare Apps for Android and iOS

Briefcase compiles BeeWare applications into native `.apk` (Android) and `.ipa` (iOS) files.

1. Setting Up Briefcase

1. Install Briefcase:

    sh

    ```
    pip install briefcase
    ```

2. Create a new BeeWare project:

    sh

    ```
    briefcase new
    cd myproject
    ```

2. Building the App for Android

1. Install dependencies:

    sh

    ```
    briefcase build android
    ```

2. Run the application on an emulator or connected device:

    sh

```
briefcase run android
```

3. The generated `.apk` file is stored in the `android/build` **directory**.

3. Building the App for iOS

1. Install iOS development tools:

```sh
xcode-select --install
```

2. Build the application:

```sh
briefcase build iOS
```

3. Run the application on an iPhone simulator:

```sh
briefcase run iOS
```

13.2 Publishing Apps to the App Store and Google Play

I. Publishing to Google Play Store (Android)

1. Preparing the App for Release

1. Update `buildozer.spec` for release mode:

   ini

   ```
   android.release = True
   ```

2. Generate a signed APK:

   sh

   ```
   buildozer -v android release
   ```

3. Sign the APK with a keystore:

   sh

   ```
   keytool -genkey -v -keystore my-release-key.jks -keyalg RSA -keysize 2048 -validity 10000 -alias mykey
   ```

4. Align and verify the APK:

sh

```
zipalign -v 4 bin/mykivyapp-1.0-release-
unsigned.apk mykivyapp-1.0-release.apk
apksigner sign --ks my-release-key.jks --
out        mykivyapp-1.0-release-signed.apk
mykivyapp-1.0-release.apk
```

2. Uploading to Google Play Console

1. Create a **Google Play Developer** account.
2. Register a new application in the **Google Play Console**.
3. Upload the signed APK under the "App Releases" section.
4. Fill in the **app description, screenshots, and category**.
5. Submit the app for review and wait for approval.

II. Publishing to Apple App Store (iOS)

1. Preparing the App for Release

1. Apple requires applications to be signed with a **developer certificate**.
2. Generate an .ipa file for iOS:

sh

```
briefcase package iOS
```

2. Uploading to App Store Connect

1. Enroll in the **Apple Developer Program**.

2. Create a new app in **App Store Connect**.

3. Upload the `.ipa` file using **Xcode** or **Transporter**:

```sh
xcrun altool --upload-app -f myapp.ipa -t
ios --apiKey APPLE_KEY --apiIssuer
ISSUER_ID
```

4. Fill in **metadata, screenshots, and privacy policies**.

5. Submit for **App Store review and approval**.

13.3 Summary

1. **Buildozer** packages Kivy apps into `.apk` for Android.

2. **Briefcase** compiles BeeWare apps into native `.apk` (Android) and `.ipa` (iOS) files.

3. The **Google Play Store** requires a **signed APK** before submission.

4. The **Apple App Store** requires a **developer certificate** and review approval.

5. Both stores require **metadata, screenshots, and privacy policy compliance** before publishing.

Next Chapter Preview: Python for Embedded and IoT Applications

1. Learn how Python is used in **IoT (Internet of Things)** applications.
2. Explore how Python runs on **Raspberry Pi and embedded devices**.
3. Build a **cross-platform IoT application** using Python.

Chapter 14

Cross-Platform Programming for IoT Devices

The **Internet of Things (IoT)** has transformed industries by enabling smart, interconnected devices. Python plays a significant role in **embedded systems and IoT development**, providing a high-level, flexible programming environment for microcontrollers, Raspberry Pi, and other IoT hardware.

In this chapter, we will:

1. Explore **Python's role in embedded systems and IoT applications**.
2. Learn how to run Python on **Raspberry Pi and microcontrollers**.

14.1 Python's Role in Embedded Systems and IoT

I. Why Use Python for IoT and Embedded Systems?

1. **Easy to Learn and Code** – Python's simplicity allows rapid prototyping and development.
2. **Cross-Platform Compatibility** – Python runs on **Windows, Linux, macOS, Raspberry Pi, and microcontrollers**.
3. **Rich Ecosystem of Libraries** – Libraries like **GPIO Zero, Adafruit CircuitPython, and MicroPython** simplify IoT development.
4. **Networking Capabilities** – Python has built-in support for **MQTT, HTTP, WebSockets**, making it ideal for IoT communication.
5. **Cloud Integration** – Python APIs easily connect IoT devices to **AWS IoT, Google Cloud IoT, and Azure IoT Hub**.

II. Types of IoT Hardware That Support Python

1. **Raspberry Pi** – Full Linux-based mini-computer with GPIO (General Purpose Input/Output) support.

2. **Microcontrollers** – Tiny low-power devices like **ESP32, ESP8266, and Arduino**, which support MicroPython.

3. **Single-Board Computers (SBCs)** – Similar to Raspberry Pi, including **BeagleBone Black, Jetson Nano**.

4. **IoT Sensors and Modules** – Temperature, motion, and humidity sensors that work with Python-based IoT applications.

14.2 Running Python on Raspberry Pi and Microcontrollers

I. Setting Up Python on Raspberry Pi

Raspberry Pi is one of the most popular platforms for running Python in IoT applications.

1. Installing Python on Raspberry Pi

1. Update the Raspberry Pi OS:

sh

```
sudo apt update && sudo apt upgrade -y
```

2. Install Python and required libraries:

sh

```
sudo apt install python3 python3-pip
```

2. Controlling GPIO Pins Using Python

1. Install **GPIO Zero**, a Python library for Raspberry Pi's GPIO pins:

sh

```
pip install gpiozero
```

2. Connect an LED to **GPIO 17** and a **ground (GND) pin** on Raspberry Pi.
3. Create a Python script (`blink.py`) to blink the LED:

python

```
from gpiozero import LED
from time import sleep

led = LED(17)   # GPIO Pin 17

while True:
    led.on()
    sleep(1)
    led.off()
```

190

```
sleep(1)
```

4. Run the script:

```sh
```

```
python3 blink.py
```

5. The LED should turn on and off every second.

3. Reading Data from a Sensor (DHT11 – Temperature & Humidity)

1. Install the required Python library:

```sh
```

```
pip install Adafruit_DHT
```

2. Read temperature and humidity data from a **DHT11 sensor:**

```python
```

```python
import Adafruit_DHT

sensor = Adafruit_DHT.DHT11
pin = 4  # GPIO pin connected to the sensor

humidity,         temperature        =
Adafruit_DHT.read_retry(sensor, pin)
```

191

```
if humidity is not None and temperature is
not None:
    print(f"Temp:          {temperature}°C
Humidity: {humidity}%")
else:
    print("Failed to retrieve data.")
```

II. Running Python on Microcontrollers (ESP32, ESP8266, Arduino)

Microcontrollers are resource-constrained devices that typically use **MicroPython or CircuitPython**, both of which are optimized for IoT.

1. Installing MicroPython on ESP32/ESP8266

1. Download **esptool** for flashing firmware:

    sh

    ```
    pip install esptool
    ```

2. Flash MicroPython firmware:

    sh

```
esptool.py --port /dev/ttyUSB0 erase_flash
esptool.py --port /dev/ttyUSB0 --baud
460800 write_flash --flash_size=detect
0x1000 esp32-20220117-v1.17.bin
```

3. Connect to the ESP32 using **REPL (Read-Eval-Print Loop)**:

```sh
sh
```

```
screen /dev/ttyUSB0 115200
```

2. Writing a Simple MicroPython Script on ESP32

1. Blink an LED using **MicroPython**:

```python
python
```

```python
from machine import Pin
import time

led = Pin(2, Pin.OUT)  # GPIO 2 on ESP32

while True:
    led.value(1)
    time.sleep(1)
    led.value(0)
    time.sleep(1)
```

3. Sending Sensor Data to the Cloud (MQTT Protocol)

1. Install **umqtt.simple** library for MQTT communication.
2. Publish sensor data to an MQTT broker:

```python
import network
import umqtt.simple as mqtt

wifi = network.WLAN(network.STA_IF)
wifi.active(True)
wifi.connect("YourSSID", "YourPassword")

broker = "mqtt.eclipse.org"
client = mqtt.MQTTClient("esp32", broker)

client.connect()
client.publish("iot/data",    "Temperature:
25°C, Humidity: 60%")
```

III. Comparing Raspberry Pi and Microcontrollers for IoT Development

Feature	Raspberry Pi	ESP32/ESP8266 (MicroPython)
Processing Power	High (Quad-core CPU)	Low (Single-core CPU)
Operating System	Full Linux OS	No OS (Runs firmware)
Power Consumption	High	Low
Use Cases	Advanced IoT, AI, Image Processing	Low-power IoT, Sensor-based Projects

14.3 Summary

1. Python is widely used in **IoT and embedded systems** due to its ease of development.

2. Raspberry Pi provides a **full-fledged Linux environment** for IoT applications.

3. MicroPython allows **Python to run on microcontrollers** like ESP32 and ESP8266.

4. Python libraries like **GPIO Zero, Adafruit DHT, and MQTT** enable hardware control and data communication.

5. IoT devices can **send data to the cloud** using MQTT or HTTP APIs.

Next Chapter Preview: Optimizing Python for Low-Power and Embedded Systems

1. Learn how to **reduce memory and CPU usage** for Python in IoT.
2. Explore **MicroPython vs. CircuitPython** for lightweight applications.
3. Implement **battery-efficient techniques** for IoT devices.

Chapter 15

Optimizing Python for Low-Power and Embedded Systems

Python is an excellent choice for **embedded systems and IoT applications**, but traditional Python (CPython) can be too resource-intensive for low-power devices. **MicroPython and CircuitPython** provide lightweight alternatives optimized for embedded systems with limited CPU power, memory, and battery life.

In this chapter, we will:

1. Explore **performance tuning techniques** for Python on low-power devices.
2. Compare **MicroPython and CircuitPython** for embedded systems.

15.1 Performance Tuning for Lightweight Devices

Embedded systems often have limited memory (RAM), CPU power, and storage. Optimizing Python code ensures smooth operation on microcontrollers and low-power processors.

I. Minimizing Memory Usage

1. **Use Integer and Boolean Data Types Instead of Floats**
   - o Floating-point operations are CPU-intensive on embedded devices.
   - o Convert floating-point calculations to integer-based computations where possible.

Example: Avoid Floating-Point Arithmetic

python

```python
# Inefficient
temperature = 23.5 * 1.8 + 32    # Uses
floating-point math

# Optimized
temperature = int(23.5 * 180 + 320) // 100
# Uses integer math
```

2. **Use Generators Instead of Lists for Large Data Sets**

o   Lists store all elements in memory, consuming RAM.

o   Generators yield values one at a time, reducing memory overhead.

Example: Using Generators for Memory Efficiency

python

```
def sensor_data():
    for i in range(1000000):
        yield i  # Generates values one at a time

for value in sensor_data():
    print(value)  # No large list stored in RAM
```

3. **Optimize String Operations**

o   Avoid string concatenation inside loops; use **join()** instead.

Example: Efficient String Handling

python

```
# Inefficient
```

199

```
message = ""
for i in range(10):
    message += str(i) + " "  # Creates new
strings in memory

# Optimized
message = " ".join(str(i) for i in
range(10))  # Uses less memory
```

II. Reducing CPU Usage

1. **Use Pre-Computed Values Instead of Repeating Calculations**
   - o Store **sensor calibration values** instead of recomputing them repeatedly.
   - o Use **lookup tables** for repetitive computations.

   Example: Lookup Table for Sensor Data

   python

   ```
   lookup = {0: 0, 1: 10, 2: 20, 3: 30}  #
   Precomputed values
   result = lookup.get(sensor_input, 0)  #
   Faster than computation
   ```

2. **Reduce Unnecessary Function Calls**

- o Inline small functions where possible to save execution time.

Example: Avoid Excessive Function Calls in Loops

python

```
# Inefficient
def get_value():
    return 42

for _ in range(1000):
    value = get_value()    # Function call
overhead

# Optimized
value = 42
for _ in range(1000):
    pass   # No redundant function calls
```

3. **Use Event-Driven Programming Instead of Polling Loops**
   - o Polling constantly checks for sensor updates, wasting CPU cycles.
   - o Use interrupts or event-driven execution.

Example: Interrupt-Based GPIO Handling

```
python

from machine import Pin

def button_pressed(pin):
    print("Button Pressed!")

button = Pin(5, Pin.IN, Pin.PULL_UP)
button.irq(trigger=Pin.IRQ_FALLING,
handler=button_pressed)
```

III. Optimizing Battery Life in IoT Devices

1. **Use Deep Sleep Mode for Microcontrollers**
   - o Deep sleep mode powers down the CPU, reducing energy consumption.
   - o Use **RTC (Real-Time Clock) timers** to wake the device when needed.

Example: Putting an ESP32 to Sleep

```
python

import machine
machine.deepsleep(10000)   # Sleep for 10
seconds
```

2. Optimize Wireless Communication

- o Wi-Fi and Bluetooth drain power significantly.
- o Use **LoRa or Zigbee** for low-power IoT communication.

Example: Turning Off Wi-Fi After Data Transmission

```python
import network

wlan = network.WLAN(network.STA_IF)
wlan.active(True)
wlan.connect("SSID", "password")

# Transmit data...
wlan.active(False)   # Disable Wi-Fi after transmission
```

3. Use Low-Power Sensors

- o Choose sensors with **low current draw**.
- o Use **I2C instead of SPI** for power efficiency.

15.2 Using MicroPython and CircuitPython

Python's standard implementation (**CPython**) is too resource-heavy for microcontrollers. **MicroPython** and **CircuitPython** are lightweight versions optimized for embedded systems.

I. MicroPython: The Lightweight Python for IoT

1. MicroPython is designed for microcontrollers like **ESP32, ESP8266, and STM32**.
2. It provides a subset of Python with additional **hardware control modules**.
3. Supports **REPL (Read-Eval-Print Loop)** for real-time testing.

Example: Blinking an LED on ESP32 Using MicroPython

```python

from machine import Pin
```

```
import time

led = Pin(2, Pin.OUT)

while True:
    led.value(1)
    time.sleep(1)
    led.value(0)
    time.sleep(1)
```

II. CircuitPython: Python for Beginners and IoT

1. CircuitPython is an adaptation of MicroPython, optimized for **Adafruit hardware**.
2. It has a simplified file system – just **drag and drop** Python files onto the board.
3. Ideal for beginners and **low-power projects**.

Example: Reading a Temperature Sensor with CircuitPython

```python
import board
import analogio
```

```
sensor = analogio.AnalogIn(board.A1)

temperature = (sensor.value * 3.3) / 65536
print("Temperature:", temperature)
```

III. Comparison of MicroPython and CircuitPython

Feature	MicroPython	CircuitPython
Best For	Advanced IoT & embedded projects	Beginners & Adafruit hardware
Hardware Support	ESP32, STM32, Raspberry Pi Pico	Adafruit boards (Feather, Gemma, Metro)
REPL Support	Yes	Yes
File System	Complex (requires MicroPython's os module)	Simple (drag-and-drop)
Power Efficiency	Optimized	Moderate

15.3 Summary

1. **Performance tuning** is crucial for running Python efficiently on low-power devices.
2. **Minimizing memory and CPU usage** improves battery life and performance.
3. **Event-driven programming** reduces unnecessary CPU load.
4. **MicroPython** is a lightweight Python version for microcontrollers like ESP32 and STM32.
5. **CircuitPython** is an easy-to-use version for Adafruit hardware, optimized for beginners.

Next Chapter Preview: Secure and Scalable IoT Applications with Python

1. Implement **secure authentication and encryption** in IoT applications.
2. Explore **cloud-based IoT platforms** for scalable device management.
3. Learn best practices for **securing Python-based IoT deployments**.

Chapter 16

Game Development with Python: Cross-Platform Possibilities

Python is widely used in game development due to its simplicity, flexibility, and extensive libraries. While it is not the primary language for AAA games, it is a popular choice for **indie games, educational tools, and game prototyping**. Several game development frameworks, such as **Pygame, Panda3D, and Godot's Python bindings**, allow developers to build cross-platform games for **Windows, macOS, Linux, and mobile devices**.

In this chapter, we will:

1. Explore **Pygame, Panda3D, and Godot's Python bindings** for game development.
2. Discuss **portability challenges** in cross-platform game development.

16.1 Overview of Pygame, Panda3D, and Godot's Python Bindings

I. Pygame: Simple and Lightweight Game Development

1. **Pygame** is a Python library designed for **2D game development**.
2. It is built on **SDL (Simple DirectMedia Layer)**, providing cross-platform support.
3. Pygame is best suited for **arcade games, platformers, and educational games**.

1. Installing Pygame

sh

```
pip install pygame
```

2. Creating a Simple Pygame Window

python

```
import pygame

pygame.init()
screen = pygame.display.set_mode((800, 600))
pygame.display.set_caption("Pygame Window")
```

```
running = True
while running:
    for event in pygame.event.get():
        if event.type == pygame.QUIT:
            running = False

pygame.quit()
```

3. Advantages of Pygame

1. **Easy to learn and use** – Ideal for beginners.
2. **Portable across Windows, macOS, and Linux.**
3. **Good for prototyping and simple games.**

4. Limitations of Pygame

1. No built-in 3D support (only **2D rendering**).
2. Performance may not be suitable for complex games.

II. Panda3D: Full-Featured 3D Game Engine

1. **Panda3D** is a powerful, open-source 3D game engine originally developed by **Disney**.
2. It supports **Windows, macOS, and Linux**.

3. Panda3D includes a **physics engine, shader support, and networking features**.

1. Installing Panda3D

sh

```
pip install panda3d
```

2. Creating a Simple Panda3D Window

python

```
from direct.showbase.ShowBase import ShowBase

class MyApp(ShowBase):
    def __init__(self):
        ShowBase.__init__(self)

app = MyApp()
app.run()
```

3. Advantages of Panda3D

1. **Built-in physics engine** for game mechanics.
2. **Support for shaders, animations, and multiplayer features**.
3. **Optimized for large-scale 3D games**.

4. Limitations of Panda3D

1. **More complex than Pygame**, requiring knowledge of 3D programming.
2. **No built-in mobile support** (needs extra work for Android/iOS).

III. Godot with Python (GDScript and Python Bindings)

1. **Godot** is a modern, open-source **2D/3D game engine**.
2. While Godot primarily uses **GDScript**, it also supports **Python via Godot-Python bindings**.
3. It can export games to **Windows, macOS, Linux, Android, iOS, and web browsers**.

1. Installing Godot-Python Bindings

1. Download **Godot** from godotengine.org.
2. Install Python bindings:

sh

```
pip install godot-python
```

2. Creating a Simple Game Scene in Godot with Python

python

```
extends Node2D

func _ready():
    print("Hello from Godot Python!")
```

3. Advantages of Godot with Python

1. **Export to desktop, mobile, and web.**
2. **Modern editor with drag-and-drop tools.**
3. **Great for indie game development.**

4. Limitations of Godot with Python

1. Python support is **not native** (uses bindings).
2. Some **performance limitations** compared to C++.

16.2 Portability Challenges in Game Development

I. Differences in Hardware and Operating Systems

1. **Input Handling:**
   o Windows uses **DirectInput/XInput** for controllers.

- o   macOS and Linux rely on **SDL or OpenGL**.
- o   Mobile games require **touchscreen support**.

2. **Performance Differences:**

- o   Windows supports **DirectX**, while macOS uses **Metal**, and Linux relies on **OpenGL/Vulkan**.
- o   Performance optimizations must account for platform-specific rendering differences.

Solution:

- Use **cross-platform libraries** like SDL (Pygame) and OpenGL (Panda3D).
- Optimize **asset loading** to avoid platform bottlenecks.

II. UI and Resolution Scaling Issues

1. Games must handle **various screen resolutions and aspect ratios**.
2. A UI designed for **1080p monitors** may not scale properly on **mobile screens**.

Solution:

- Use **relative layout scaling** instead of fixed pixel sizes.
- Implement **dynamic resolution settings** to adjust based on the device.

III. Mobile vs. Desktop Controls

1. Desktop games use **keyboard and mouse**.
2. Mobile games require **touch controls and accelerometer support**.
3. Console games need **gamepad integration**.

Solution:

- Use **event-driven input handling** to support multiple control schemes.
- Implement **custom touch gestures** for mobile interfaces.

IV. Deployment and Distribution Challenges

1. **Windows, macOS, and Linux** require different **packaging formats** (EXE, DMG, AppImage).
2. **iOS and Android** have strict **app store submission guidelines**.
3. **Web-based games** require **WebGL** compatibility.

Solution:

- Use **PyInstaller** to bundle Pygame/Panda3D games for desktop:

```sh
pyinstaller --onefile game.py
```

- Use **Godot's built-in export tools** to package games for multiple platforms.
- Optimize for **WebGL** when targeting browser-based games.

16.3 Summary

1. **Pygame** is ideal for 2D games and beginner-friendly game development.
2. **Panda3D** offers **advanced 3D capabilities** but requires optimization for mobile.
3. **Godot with Python bindings** provides **a modern, cross-platform engine**.
4. Cross-platform challenges include **hardware differences, UI scaling, input handling, and packaging for distribution**.
5. **Cross-platform libraries and careful optimizations** ensure smooth performance across devices.

Next Chapter Preview: Advanced Game Physics and AI with Python

1. Implement **game physics** using Pygame and Panda3D.
2. Explore **AI-based game mechanics** using Python libraries.
3. Optimize **pathfinding and enemy behavior** in games.

Chapter 17

Building a Simple Cross-Platform Game

Developing a cross-platform game requires careful consideration of performance, input handling, and resource management. **Pygame**, a popular Python game development library, is an excellent choice for building lightweight 2D games that run on **Windows, macOS, and Linux**.

In this chapter, we will:

1. Create a **hands-on 2D game project** using **Pygame**.
2. Optimize the game's **performance for different platforms**.

17.1 Hands-On Project: Creating a 2D Game with Pygame

We will develop a **simple cross-platform game**: **"Alien Shooter"**, where the player controls a spaceship that shoots at falling alien ships.

I. Setting Up the Game Environment

1. Installing Pygame

Before starting, install Pygame using pip:

```sh
pip install pygame
```

2. Creating the Game Window

1. Create a new file `alien_shooter.py` and set up the game window:

```python
import pygame

# Initialize Pygame
```

```
pygame.init()

# Set screen dimensions
SCREEN_WIDTH, SCREEN_HEIGHT = 800, 600
screen = pygame.display.set_mode((SCREEN_WIDTH,
SCREEN_HEIGHT))

# Set window title
pygame.display.set_caption("Alien Shooter")

# Main game loop
running = True
while running:
    for event in pygame.event.get():
        if event.type == pygame.QUIT:
            running = False

    # Fill screen with black color
    screen.fill((0, 0, 0))

    # Update display
    pygame.display.flip()

# Quit Pygame
pygame.quit()
```

2. Run the script:

```sh
sh
```

```
python alien_shooter.py
```

This will open a **black game window**, ready for further development.

II. Adding Player and Alien Sprites

We will now add:

1. A **spaceship controlled by the player.**
2. **Aliens that fall from the top.**

1. Creating a Spaceship Class

python

```
class Spaceship(pygame.sprite.Sprite):
    def __init__(self):
        super().__init__()
        self.image                             =
pygame.image.load("spaceship.png")     # Load a
spaceship image
        self.rect                              =
self.image.get_rect(midbottom=(SCREEN_WIDTH   //
2, SCREEN_HEIGHT - 50))
        self.speed = 5
```

```python
    def update(self, keys):
        if          keys[pygame.K_LEFT]          and
self.rect.left > 0:
            self.rect.x -= self.speed
        if          keys[pygame.K_RIGHT]          and
self.rect.right < SCREEN_WIDTH:
            self.rect.x += self.speed
```

2. Creating an Alien Class

python

```python
import random

class Alien(pygame.sprite.Sprite):
    def __init__(self):
        super().__init__()
        self.image                              =
pygame.image.load("alien.png")   # Load an alien
image
        self.rect                               =
self.image.get_rect(midtop=(random.randint(0,
SCREEN_WIDTH), 0))
        self.speed = random.randint(2, 5)

    def update(self):
        self.rect.y += self.speed
        if self.rect.top > SCREEN_HEIGHT:
            self.kill()   # Remove alien if it
goes off-screen
```

III. Handling Player Input and Shooting

1. Modify the **main game loop** to handle player movement and shooting:

python

```python
# Load spaceship sprite
spaceship = Spaceship()
all_sprites = pygame.sprite.Group(spaceship)
aliens = pygame.sprite.Group()

# Clock for controlling frame rate
clock = pygame.time.Clock()

running = True
while running:
    # Handle events
    for event in pygame.event.get():
        if event.type == pygame.QUIT:
            running = False

    # Get key presses
    keys = pygame.key.get_pressed()
    spaceship.update(keys)

    # Spawn aliens randomly
```

```
if random.randint(1, 50) == 1:
    alien = Alien()
    all_sprites.add(alien)
    aliens.add(alien)

# Update sprites
all_sprites.update()

# Draw everything
screen.fill((0, 0, 0))
all_sprites.draw(screen)
pygame.display.flip()

# Limit frame rate
clock.tick(60)

pygame.quit()
```

Now, the spaceship can **move left and right**, and aliens **fall from the top** at random intervals.

IV. Adding a Shooting Mechanism

1. Create a **Bullet Class**:

```
python
```

```
class Bullet(pygame.sprite.Sprite):
    def __init__(self, x, y):
        super().__init__()
        self.image = pygame.Surface((5, 20))
        self.image.fill((255, 255, 255))
        self.rect                        =
self.image.get_rect(midbottom=(x, y))
        self.speed = -8

    def update(self):
        self.rect.y += self.speed
        if self.rect.bottom < 0:
            self.kill()   # Remove bullet if it
goes off-screen
```

2. Modify the game loop to allow **shooting bullets**:

python

```
bullets = pygame.sprite.Group()

while running:
    for event in pygame.event.get():
        if event.type == pygame.QUIT:
            running = False

        # Shoot a bullet when SPACE is pressed
        if event.type == pygame.KEYDOWN and
event.key == pygame.K_SPACE:
```

```
        bullet                      =
Bullet(spaceship.rect.centerx,
spaceship.rect.top)
            all_sprites.add(bullet)
            bullets.add(bullet)

    # Check for bullet-alien collisions
    for bullet in bullets:
        hit_aliens                      =
pygame.sprite.spritecollide(bullet,        aliens,
True)
        if hit_aliens:
            bullet.kill()  # Remove bullet if it
hits an alien

    # Update and draw sprites
    all_sprites.update()
    screen.fill((0, 0, 0))
    all_sprites.draw(screen)
    pygame.display.flip()
    clock.tick(60)

pygame.quit()
```

Now, pressing the **SPACEBAR** will shoot bullets that destroy aliens on impact!

17.2 Optimizing Performance for Different Platforms

Cross-platform games must be optimized for **frame rate, input handling, and graphics rendering.**

I. Improving Performance in Pygame

1. **Use a Game Clock to Limit FPS**
   - o Prevents unnecessary CPU usage.

   python

   ```python
   clock = pygame.time.Clock()
   while running:
       clock.tick(60)  # Limit to 60 FPS
   ```

2. **Reduce Screen Updates**
   - o Only update areas that change instead of redrawing the entire screen.

   python

   ```python
   pygame.display.update(spaceship.rect)
   ```

3. **Optimize Collision Detection**

- o Instead of checking every bullet against every alien, use **sprite groups** for efficiency.

python

```
pygame.sprite.spritecollide(bullet,
aliens, True)
```

II. Exporting for Different Platforms

1. **Windows/macOS/Linux**
   - o Use **PyInstaller** to create an executable file:

sh

```
pyinstaller --onefile alien_shooter.py
```

2. **Android/iOS (Kivy Alternative)**
   - o Convert the game using **Kivy** and package it with **Buildozer**.

17.3 Summary

1. We built a **simple 2D game** using **Pygame**.
2. The game features **a spaceship, falling aliens, and shooting mechanics**.

3. We optimized **game performance** by **limiting FPS, reducing screen updates, and optimizing collision detection.**

4. We explored **cross-platform packaging** for **Windows, macOS, Linux, and Android.**

Next Chapter Preview: Advanced Game Mechanics with AI and Physics

1. Implement **game physics (gravity, collisions, bouncing effects).**

2. Introduce **AI-controlled enemies with pathfinding and decision-making.**

3. Optimize large-scale games using **multithreading and procedural generation.**

Chapter 18

Python for System Automation and Scripting

Python is a powerful tool for **automating repetitive tasks** and **writing system scripts** that work across multiple platforms. Its standard library provides modules that allow interaction with **Windows, macOS, and Linux**, enabling developers to create **universal automation scripts**.

In this chapter, we will:

1. Learn how to **automate system tasks on Windows, macOS, and Linux**.
2. Write **cross-platform scripts** that work seamlessly across all operating systems.

18.1 Automating Tasks on Windows, macOS, and Linux

Python allows system-level automation through built-in modules such as **os, subprocess, shutil, and pathlib**.

I. File and Directory Management

Managing files and directories is essential for system scripting. Python provides cross-platform methods for:

1. **Creating, moving, renaming, and deleting files/directories.**
2. **Checking file properties and permissions.**

1. Creating and Deleting Directories
python

```
import os

# Create a new directory
os.makedirs("new_folder", exist_ok=True)

# Remove directory (only if empty)
os.rmdir("new_folder")
```

2. Listing Files in a Directory

```python
import os

# List all files in a directory
for file in os.listdir("."):
    print(file)
```

3. Moving and Renaming Files

```python
import shutil

# Move file
shutil.move("source.txt", "destination_folder/")

# Rename file
os.rename("old_name.txt", "new_name.txt")
```

II. Running System Commands with Python

Python can execute system commands using **subprocess**, allowing automation of administrative tasks.

1. Running Shell Commands (Cross-Platform Approach)

```python
```

```
import subprocess

# Run a system command
result    =    subprocess.run(["ls",    "-l"],
capture_output=True, text=True)
print(result.stdout)
```

2. Running Different Commands Based on the OS

```
python

import os
import subprocess

if os.name == "nt":   # Windows
    subprocess.run(["dir"], shell=True)
else:   # macOS/Linux
    subprocess.run(["ls", "-la"])
```

III. Scheduling Automated Tasks

Python can schedule scripts to run **automatically** at specific times using **Windows Task Scheduler, cron (Linux/macOS), and the schedule library**.

1. Using Python's schedule Library

```
python

import schedule
```

233

```python
import time

def task():
    print("Automated task running...")

# Run task every minute
schedule.every(1).minutes.do(task)

while True:
    schedule.run_pending()
    time.sleep(1)
```

2. Scheduling Tasks on Windows (Task Scheduler)

1. Open **Task Scheduler** and create a new task.

2. Set the trigger to **run at a specified time**.

3. Set the action to **run Python with the script**:

   sh

   ```
   python C:\path\to\script.py
   ```

3. Scheduling Tasks on macOS/Linux (Cron Jobs)

1. Open the terminal and type:

   sh

   ```
   crontab -e
   ```

2. Add a cron job to run the script every hour:

```sh
sh

0    *    *    *    *        /usr/bin/python3
/home/user/script.py
```

18.2 Writing Universal Scripts That Work Everywhere

Cross-platform automation requires **portable scripts** that work on Windows, macOS, and Linux.

I. Detecting the Operating System

Python's `platform` module helps determine the OS before executing system-specific commands.

```python
python

import platform

os_name = platform.system()

if os_name == "Windows":
    print("Running on Windows")
elif os_name == "Darwin":
    print("Running on macOS")
```

235

```
elif os_name == "Linux":
    print("Running on Linux")
```

II. Using `pathlib` for Cross-Platform File Paths

Instead of using platform-specific paths (`C:\Users\` for Windows, `/home/user/` for Linux/macOS), use `pathlib`.

python

```
from pathlib import Path

# Get the home directory (works on all platforms)
home = Path.home()
print(home)

# Create a cross-platform path
file_path = home / "Documents" / "script.py"
print(file_path)
```

III. Automating File Backups Across Platforms

The following script **copies important files** from a specified directory to a backup location, working across **Windows, macOS, and Linux**.

```python
import shutil
from pathlib import Path

# Define source and backup directories
source_dir = Path.home() / "Documents" / "important_files"
backup_dir = Path.home() / "Documents" / "backup"

# Create backup directory if it doesn't exist
backup_dir.mkdir(parents=True, exist_ok=True)

# Copy files
for file in source_dir.glob("*"):
    shutil.copy(file, backup_dir / file.name)

print("Backup completed successfully.")
```

IV. Automating System Updates and Cleanup

Python can help keep systems clean by automating updates and removing unnecessary files.

1. Windows: Clearing Temporary Files

```python
```

```python
import os
import shutil

temp_folder = os.getenv("TEMP")
shutil.rmtree(temp_folder, ignore_errors=True)
print("Temporary files deleted.")
```

2. Linux/macOS: Running System Updates

```python
```

```python
import subprocess

# Linux/macOS system update
subprocess.run(["sudo", "apt-get", "update"],
check=True)
subprocess.run(["sudo", "apt-get", "upgrade", "-
y"], check=True)
print("System updated successfully.")
```

18.3 Summary

1. **Python enables automation** of system tasks like **file management, scheduling, and system updates.**

2. **Subprocess** allows **executing system commands** across different platforms.

3. **Scheduling with** `schedule`, **Task Scheduler (Windows), and cron jobs (Linux/macOS)** enables periodic execution.

4. **Using** `platform` **and** `pathlib` ensures that scripts work across **Windows, macOS, and Linux.**

5. **Python can automate backups, cleanup tasks, and system updates**, enhancing productivity.

Next Chapter Preview: Automating Cloud Workflows with Python

1. Automate **AWS, Google Cloud, and Azure** using Python APIs.

2. Use **Boto3, Google Cloud SDK, and Azure SDK** for cloud management.

3. Deploy scripts for **serverless automation and cloud resource management**.

Chapter 19

Cross-Platform CLI and Terminal Applications

Command-line interfaces (CLI) are essential for automating tasks, managing system processes, and interacting with cloud services. Python provides powerful libraries such as **argparse, Click, and Typer** to create user-friendly, cross-platform terminal applications.

In this chapter, we will:

1. Build **command-line interfaces (CLI) using argparse, Click, and Typer**.
2. Learn how to **make scripts executable on Windows, macOS, and Linux**.

19.1 Building Command-Line Interfaces with argparse, Click, and Typer

Python offers multiple ways to create CLI applications, ranging from **basic argument parsing** to **advanced interactive applications**.

I. Using argparse: The Standard Python Library for CLI

`argparse` is a built-in Python module for handling command-line arguments.

1. Creating a Basic CLI with argparse

```python
python

import argparse

# Create the parser
parser                                    =
argparse.ArgumentParser(description="Simple   CLI
Application")

# Add arguments
parser.add_argument("name", help="Your name")
```

241

```
parser.add_argument("--age",           type=int,
help="Your age", required=False)

# Parse arguments
args = parser.parse_args()

# Display output
print(f"Hello, {args.name}!")
if args.age:
    print(f"You are {args.age} years old.")
```

2. Running the Script

```
sh
```

```
python cli_script.py Alice --age 30
```

3. Advantages of argparse

1. **Built into Python (no additional installation required).**
2. **Supports positional and optional arguments.**
3. **Great for small and medium CLI applications.**

II. Using Click: A More User-Friendly CLI Library

Click is a third-party Python library designed for creating **intuitive** and **structured** CLI applications.

1. Installing Click

sh

```
pip install click
```

2. Creating a Click-Based CLI

python

```
import click

@click.command()
@click.option("--name",    prompt="Your    name",
help="Enter your name")
@click.option("--age",  default=25,  help="Enter
your age")
def greet(name, age):
    click.echo(f"Hello,  {name}!  You  are  {age}
years old.")

if __name__ == "__main__":
    greet()
```

3. Running the Click-Based CLI

sh

```
python cli_script.py --name Alice --age 30
```

4. Advantages of Click

1. **Better user experience** with prompts and error handling.
2. **Supports subcommands** for complex CLI applications.

3. **Requires less boilerplate code than argparse.**

III. Using Typer: A Modern, Fast CLI Library Based on Python Type Hints

Typer is a **fast and easy-to-use** CLI framework built on `Click`. It leverages Python **type hints** to simplify command-line applications.

1. Installing Typer

sh

```
pip install typer
```

2. Creating a CLI with Typer

python

```
import typer

app = typer.Typer()

@app.command()
def greet(name: str, age: int = 25):
    """Greet the user with their name and age."""
    typer.echo(f"Hello, {name}! You are {age}
years old.")
```

```
if __name__ == "__main__":
    app()
```

3. Running the Typer-Based CLI

```sh
sh
```

```
python cli_script.py greet Alice --age 30
```

4. Advantages of Typer

1. **Simplifies CLI development** using Python's type hints.

2. **Automatically generates help documentation.**

3. **Ideal for building APIs and interactive terminal applications.**

19.2 Making Scripts Executable on All Platforms

To make Python scripts executable across Windows, macOS, and Linux, follow these best practices.

I. Making a Python Script Executable on Linux/macOS

1. Add a **shebang** at the top of the script:

```
python
```

```
#!/usr/bin/env python3
```

2. Change file permissions to make it executable:

```
sh
```

```
chmod +x cli_script.py
```

3. Run the script directly:

```
sh
```

```
./cli_script.py --name Alice --age 30
```

II. Making a Python Script Executable on Windows

1. **Create a batch file** (`cli_script.bat`):

```
bat
```

```
@echo off
python cli_script.py %*
```

2. Place the `.bat` file in a system PATH directory to run it globally.

III. Creating a Standalone Executable for Any OS

Python scripts can be converted into standalone executables using **PyInstaller**.

1. Install PyInstaller:

    sh

    ```
    pip install pyinstaller
    ```

2. Generate an executable:

    sh

    ```
    pyinstaller --onefile cli_script.py
    ```

3. The executable will be created inside the `dist/` directory.

IV. Packaging the Executable for Different Platforms

Platform	Packaging Tool	Command
Windows	PyInstaller	`pyinstaller --onefile cli_script.py`

Platform	Packaging Tool	Command
macOS	PyInstaller	`pyinstaller --onefile cli_script.py`
Linux	chmod +x	`chmod +x cli_script.py`

19.3 Summary

1. **argparse** is built into Python and is great for simple CLI tools.

2. **Click** provides an interactive and user-friendly experience for CLI applications.

3. **Typer** is ideal for modern CLI tools using **Python type hints**.

4. Scripts can be made **executable across platforms** using `chmod +x` (Linux/macOS) or `.bat` files (Windows).

5. **PyInstaller** enables conversion of Python scripts into standalone executables.

Next Chapter Preview: Automating Cloud Workflows with Python

1. Automate AWS, Google Cloud, and Azure using Python APIs.

2. Use **Boto3, Google Cloud SDK, and Azure SDK** for cloud resource management.

3. Deploy scripts for **serverless automation and cloud orchestration**.

Chapter 20

Concurrency and Parallelism for High-Performance Applications

Concurrency and parallelism are essential for building high-performance applications that **handle multiple tasks simultaneously**. Python provides several techniques to improve efficiency, including **multithreading, multiprocessing, and asynchronous programming** with **asyncio**.

In this chapter, we will:

1. Compare **multiprocessing vs. multithreading** and when to use each.
2. Explore **asyncio and cooperative multitasking** for efficient, non-blocking operations.

20.1 Multiprocessing vs. Multithreading

I. Understanding the Global Interpreter Lock (GIL)

1. Python's **Global Interpreter Lock (GIL)** allows only one thread to execute Python bytecode at a time.
2. This means **multithreading does not improve performance** for CPU-bound tasks.
3. **Multiprocessing bypasses the GIL** by running tasks in separate processes.

II. Multithreading: Ideal for I/O-Bound Tasks

Best for:

1. **I/O-bound tasks** (e.g., network requests, file I/O, database queries).
2. Applications that spend time **waiting** for external resources.

Example: Running Multiple Threads with Python's `threading` Module

```python
python

import threading
import time

def worker():
    print("Worker started")
    time.sleep(2)
    print("Worker finished")

# Create and start threads
thread1 = threading.Thread(target=worker)
thread2 = threading.Thread(target=worker)

thread1.start()
thread2.start()

thread1.join()
thread2.join()

print("All threads completed")
```

Key Features of Multithreading:

1. Threads **share memory** within a single Python process.
2. **Best for tasks involving network calls, database queries, or disk operations.**
3. Threads **cannot run CPU-bound tasks efficiently due to the GIL.**

III. Multiprocessing: Ideal for CPU-Bound Tasks

Best for:

1. **CPU-intensive tasks** (e.g., image processing, data analysis, machine learning).
2. Applications that need **parallel execution across multiple CPU cores**.

Example: Running Multiple Processes with Python's multiprocessing Module

```python
python

import multiprocessing
import time

def worker():
    print("Worker started")
    time.sleep(2)
    print("Worker finished")

# Create and start processes
```

```
process1                                    =
multiprocessing.Process(target=worker)
process2                                    =
multiprocessing.Process(target=worker)

process1.start()
process2.start()

process1.join()
process2.join()

print("All processes completed")
```

Key Features of Multiprocessing:

1. Processes **do not share memory** (each has its own memory space).

2. **Ideal for CPU-heavy computations** like image processing or encryption.

3. **Avoids Python's GIL**, making full use of multiple CPU cores.

IV. When to Use Multithreading vs. Multiprocessing

254

Feature	Multithreading	Multiprocessing
Best For	I/O-bound tasks	CPU-bound tasks
Execution Model	Runs multiple threads in one process	Runs separate processes
Memory Sharing	Yes (shared memory)	No (separate memory)
GIL Limitation	Affected by GIL	Bypasses GIL
Use Cases	Network requests, database queries	Data processing, machine learning

20.2 Asyncio and Cooperative Multitasking

I. What is Asyncio?

1. **Asyncio** enables **asynchronous execution** using the `async` and `await` **keywords**.
2. Unlike multithreading/multiprocessing, asyncio uses a **single thread** but efficiently switches between tasks.

3. It is **ideal for high-performance I/O-bound applications** (e.g., web scraping, real-time messaging).

II. Using Asyncio for Asynchronous Execution

Example: Running Asynchronous Functions with `asyncio`

```python
import asyncio

async def worker():
    print("Worker started")
    await asyncio.sleep(2)  # Non-blocking sleep
    print("Worker finished")

async def main():
    await asyncio.gather(worker(), worker())  # Run tasks concurrently

asyncio.run(main())
```

III. Asyncio vs. Multithreading vs. Multiprocessing

Feature	Asyncio	Multithreading	Multiprocessing
Best For	I/O-bound tasks	I/O-bound tasks	CPU-bound tasks
Execution Model	Single-threaded, event-driven	Multi-threaded	Multi-process
GIL Impact	Avoids GIL issues	Affected by GIL	Bypasses GIL
Performance Benefit	Reduces idle time (efficient switching)	Parallel I/O execution	True parallel execution

IV. Asyncio Example: Fetching Multiple Web Pages

```python

import asyncio
import aiohttp

async def fetch(url):
```

```
        async    with    aiohttp.ClientSession()    as
session:
            async with session.get(url) as response:
                return await response.text()

async def main():
    urls          =              ["https://example.com",
"https://python.org"]
    results = await asyncio.gather(*(fetch(url)
for url in urls))
    print(results)

asyncio.run(main())
```

20.3 Summary

1. **Multithreading** is best for **I/O-bound tasks** like network requests and database queries.

2. **Multiprocessing** is best for **CPU-bound tasks**, as it bypasses Python's GIL.

3. **Asyncio** is ideal for **high-performance, single-threaded, event-driven applications**.

4. Choosing between **asyncio, threading, and multiprocessing** depends on the task type:

   o **Use multithreading** for tasks waiting on external resources.

- o **Use multiprocessing** for tasks requiring heavy computation.
- o **Use asyncio** for non-blocking, scalable network applications.

Next Chapter Preview: Secure and Scalable Python Applications

1. Implement **secure authentication and encryption** in Python applications.
2. Explore **best practices for secure Python development**.
3. Learn **scalability techniques** for cloud-based Python applications.

Chapter 21

Cross-Platform Databases and Data Persistence

Modern applications require efficient data storage and retrieval mechanisms that work seamlessly across **Windows, macOS, and Linux**. Python provides a variety of database solutions, including **relational databases (SQLite, PostgreSQL)** and **NoSQL databases (MongoDB, Firebase)**.

In this chapter, we will:

1. Explore **SQLite, PostgreSQL, and NoSQL databases** for cross-platform data storage.
2. Use **Object-Relational Mappers (ORMs)** like **SQLAlchemy and Django ORM** to simplify database interactions.

21.1 SQLite, PostgreSQL, and NoSQL for Universal Storage

Python applications require flexible storage solutions that work across multiple platforms.

I. SQLite: Lightweight, Built-In Database

1. **SQLite** is a **serverless, self-contained** SQL database that comes pre-installed with Python.
2. It is ideal for **small to medium applications** that do not require a separate database server.
3. SQLite **stores data in a single** `.db` **file,** making it highly portable.

1. Using SQLite in Python

python

```
import sqlite3

# Connect to the database (or create it if it
doesn't exist)
conn = sqlite3.connect("database.db")
cursor = conn.cursor()
```

```python
# Create a table
cursor.execute("""
    CREATE TABLE IF NOT EXISTS users (
        id INTEGER PRIMARY KEY,
        name TEXT,
        age INTEGER
    )
""")

# Insert data
cursor.execute("INSERT INTO users (name, age)
VALUES (?, ?)", ("Alice", 25))
conn.commit()

# Fetch data
cursor.execute("SELECT * FROM users")
print(cursor.fetchall())

# Close connection
conn.close()
```

2. Advantages of SQLite

1. **No installation required** (built into Python).

2. **Cross-platform and lightweight** (single .db file).

3. Ideal for **local applications and mobile apps**.

3. Limitations of SQLite

1. **Not suitable for high-traffic applications.**
2. **Limited concurrency** (single writer at a time).
3. Lacks advanced features like **replication and partitioning**.

II. PostgreSQL: Scalable Relational Database

1. **PostgreSQL** is a powerful, cross-platform **relational database** suited for high-performance applications.
2. Supports **concurrent transactions, replication, and advanced indexing.**
3. Ideal for **web applications, enterprise applications, and cloud-based solutions.**

1. Installing PostgreSQL and Psycopg2 Driver

sh

```
pip install psycopg2
```

2. Connecting to PostgreSQL in Python

python

```python
import psycopg2

# Connect to PostgreSQL
conn = psycopg2.connect(
    dbname="mydatabase",
    user="myuser",
    password="mypassword",
    host="localhost",
    port="5432"
)
cursor = conn.cursor()

# Create a table
cursor.execute("""
    CREATE TABLE IF NOT EXISTS users (
        id SERIAL PRIMARY KEY,
        name TEXT,
        age INTEGER
    )
""")

# Insert data
cursor.execute("INSERT INTO users (name, age)
VALUES (%s, %s)", ("Bob", 30))
conn.commit()

# Fetch data
cursor.execute("SELECT * FROM users")
print(cursor.fetchall())
```

```
# Close connection
conn.close()
```

3. Advantages of PostgreSQL

1. **Full SQL support** with advanced features.

2. **Highly scalable and concurrent** (supports multiple users).

3. **Cross-platform support** (Windows, macOS, Linux, and cloud).

4. Limitations of PostgreSQL

1. **Requires installation** (not built into Python).

2. **More complex setup** compared to SQLite.

III. NoSQL: MongoDB for Document-Based Storage

1. **MongoDB** is a NoSQL database that stores data in **JSON-like documents** instead of tables.

2. **Best for dynamic data**, high scalability, and cloud-based applications.

3. **Supports flexible schemas**, making it ideal for IoT, big data, and real-time analytics.

1. Installing MongoDB and PyMongo

sh

```
pip install pymongo
```

2. Connecting to MongoDB and Inserting Documents

python

```
from pymongo import MongoClient

# Connect to MongoDB
client                                    =
MongoClient("mongodb://localhost:27017/")
db = client.mydatabase

# Insert data
db.users.insert_one({"name":  "Charlie",  "age":
35})

# Fetch data
for user in db.users.find():
    print(user)
```

3. Advantages of MongoDB

1. **Schema-less (flexible data structure).**
2. **High scalability** (supports horizontal scaling).

3. **Ideal for real-time applications and unstructured data.**

4. Limitations of MongoDB

1. **Lacks ACID transactions** (compared to SQL databases).
2. **More storage space required** than relational databases.

21.2 Using ORMs like SQLAlchemy and Django ORM

Interacting with databases using **raw SQL queries** can be error-prone and repetitive. **Object-Relational Mappers (ORMs)** allow developers to use Python objects instead of writing SQL manually.

I. SQLAlchemy: Universal ORM for Python

SQLAlchemy supports **SQLite, PostgreSQL, MySQL, and more**, making it highly versatile.

1. Installing SQLAlchemy

sh

```
pip install sqlalchemy
```

2. Defining a Database Model in SQLAlchemy

```
python
```

```python
from sqlalchemy import create_engine, Column,
Integer, String
from      sqlalchemy.ext.declarative      import
declarative_base
from sqlalchemy.orm import sessionmaker

# Connect to SQLite database
engine = create_engine("sqlite:///database.db")
Base = declarative_base()

# Define a User model
class User(Base):
    __tablename__ = "users"
    id = Column(Integer, primary_key=True)
    name = Column(String)
    age = Column(Integer)


Base.metadata.create_all(engine)

# Insert and query data
Session = sessionmaker(bind=engine)
session = Session()
new_user = User(name="Alice", age=25)
session.add(new_user)
session.commit()
```

```
for user in session.query(User).all():
    print(user.name, user.age)
```

3. Advantages of SQLAlchemy

1. **Works with multiple databases (SQLite, PostgreSQL, MySQL, etc.).**
2. **Prevents SQL injection** by using parameterized queries.
3. **Simplifies database migrations** and schema changes.

II. Django ORM: ORM for Web Applications

1. **Django ORM** is built into Django for **database management in web applications**.
2. Supports **automatic table creation, migrations, and querying**.

1. Defining a Model in Django ORM

```python
python

from django.db import models

class User(models.Model):
    name = models.CharField(max_length=100)
```

269

```
age = models.IntegerField()
```

2. Querying Data in Django ORM

python

```
# Fetch all users
users = User.objects.all()


# Filter users by age
young_users = User.objects.filter(age__lt=30)
```

3. Advantages of Django ORM

1. **Integrated with Django web framework.**

2. **Supports database migrations** automatically.

3. **Easy-to-use API for querying data.**

21.3 Summary

1. **SQLite** is ideal for lightweight, local databases.

2. **PostgreSQL** is best for high-performance relational databases.

3. **MongoDB** is useful for **NoSQL, flexible schema applications**.

4. **SQLAlchemy** provides a **universal ORM** for multiple databases.

5. **Django ORM** is best for **web applications** requiring database integration.

Next Chapter Preview: Secure and Scalable Python Applications

1. Learn **best practices for securing database connections**.
2. Implement **authentication, encryption, and access controls**.
3. Scale Python applications using **caching, indexing, and cloud databases**.

Chapter 22

Security Best Practices for Cross-Platform Applications

Security is a crucial consideration when developing **cross-platform applications**. Applications that run on **Windows, macOS, Linux, and mobile devices** must implement **strong authentication, encryption, and secure coding principles** to protect sensitive data and prevent vulnerabilities.

In this chapter, we will:

- Learn **authentication, encryption, and secure coding best practices**.
- Explore **techniques to prevent vulnerabilities** in cross-platform applications.

22.1 Handling Authentication, Encryption, and Secure Coding Principles

I. Secure Authentication for Applications

1. **Use Secure Password Hashing**

    1. Never store passwords in plaintext.

    2. Use **bcrypt, Argon2, or PBKDF2** for hashing.

Example: Hashing a Password with bcrypt

```python
python

import bcrypt

password = b"securepassword"
hashed     =     bcrypt.hashpw(password,
bcrypt.gensalt())

print("Hashed password:", hashed)
```

2. **Implement Multi-Factor Authentication (MFA)**

    1. Use **Time-based One-Time Passwords (TOTP)** for added security.

Example: Generating OTP with PyOTP

```python
python

import pyotp

secret = pyotp.random_base32()
totp = pyotp.TOTP(secret)
print("Your OTP:", totp.now())
```

3. OAuth2 and API Authentication

1. For web and API-based applications, use **OAuth2** with libraries like `authlib`.

2. Implement token-based authentication with **JWT (JSON Web Tokens)**.

Example: Generating a JWT Token

```python
python

import jwt
import datetime

secret_key = "supersecret"
payload = {"user": "Alice", "exp":
datetime.datetime.utcnow()            +
datetime.timedelta(hours=1)}
token = jwt.encode(payload, secret_key,
algorithm="HS256")

print("JWT Token:", token)
```

II. Encryption and Secure Data Storage

1. Use AES Encryption for Data Protection

- o AES (Advanced Encryption Standard) is a secure encryption algorithm.

Example: Encrypting and Decrypting Data with AES

```python
from cryptography.fernet import Fernet

key = Fernet.generate_key()
cipher = Fernet(key)

encrypted_text                    =
cipher.encrypt(b"Sensitive Data")
decrypted_text                    =
cipher.decrypt(encrypted_text)

print("Decrypted                  Data:",
decrypted_text.decode())
```

2. Secure Database Connections

- o Always use **SSL/TLS** when connecting to remote databases.
- o Use **environment variables** for storing database credentials instead of hardcoding them.

Example: Connecting Securely to PostgreSQL

275

```python
python

import psycopg2
import os

conn = psycopg2.connect(
    dbname="mydb",
    user=os.getenv("DB_USER"),
    password=os.getenv("DB_PASS"),
    host="db.example.com",
    sslmode="require"
)
```

3. **Encrypt Sensitive Data at Rest**
   - For file storage, use **encrypted disk partitions** or **file encryption tools**.
   - For cloud storage, ensure **data is encrypted before transmission**.

III. Secure Coding Practices

1. **Avoid Hardcoding Secrets**
   - Store API keys, passwords, and tokens in **environment variables or vaults**.

Example: Using Environment Variables for Secrets

```python
import os

api_key = os.getenv("API_KEY")
```

2. **Sanitize User Inputs to Prevent Injection Attacks**
   - Always use **parameterized queries** when interacting with databases.

Example: Preventing SQL Injection

```python
cursor.execute("SELECT * FROM users WHERE username = %s", (username,))
```

3. **Validate User Inputs**
   - Use **input validation** to prevent **buffer overflow, command injection, and XSS attacks**.

Example: Validating Email Input with Regex

```python
import re
```

```
email = "user@example.com"
if re.match(r"[^@]+@[^@]+\.[^@]+", email):
    print("Valid email")
else:
    print("Invalid email")
```

22.2 Preventing Vulnerabilities in Cross-Platform Environments

Cross-platform applications face unique security challenges due to different OS architectures and configurations.

I. Secure File Permissions and Access Control

1. **Limit File and Folder Access**
   o Use **least privilege** principles for file access.

   Example: Setting File Permissions on Linux/macOS

   sh

   chmod 600 sensitive_file.txt

2. **Use Python's `os` and `pathlib` for Safe File Operations**

   o Prevent directory traversal attacks by using **absolute paths**.

   Example: Securely Opening Files

   ```python
   from pathlib import Path

   safe_path                              =
   Path("/secure/directory").joinpath("confi
   g.json").resolve()
   ```

II. Network Security: Secure API Calls and Communication

1. **Always Use HTTPS Instead of HTTP**

   o Use **TLS encryption** to prevent data interception.

   Example: Making Secure API Requests with `requests`

   ```python
   ```

```
import requests

response                                =
requests.get("https://api.example.com/dat
a", verify=True)
print(response.json())
```

2. Prevent Man-in-the-Middle (MITM) Attacks

o Use **certificate pinning** to validate trusted servers.

III. Sandboxing and Container Security

1. Use Virtual Environments for Python Applications

sh

```
python -m venv myenv
source myenv/bin/activate  # Linux/macOS
myenv\Scripts\activate  # Windows
```

2. Run Applications in Containers (Docker)

sh

```
docker run --read-only -it python:3.9
```

IV. Logging and Monitoring for Security Events

1. Implement Logging for Security Events

- o Use **log rotation** to prevent log overflow.

Example: Logging User Actions Securely

```python

import logging

logging.basicConfig(filename="security.lo
g", level=logging.INFO)
logging.info("User     login     attempt
detected.")
```

2. Use a SIEM (Security Information and Event Management) System

- o Integrate logs with **Splunk, ELK Stack, or AWS CloudWatch** for real-time monitoring.

V. Secure Software Distribution for Cross-Platform Apps

1. **Sign Executables and Packages**
   - o Use **code signing** to verify application integrity.

   Example: Signing a Windows Executable

   ```sh
   ```

   ```sh
   signtool        sign        /a        /t
   http://timestamp.digicert.com myapp.exe
   ```

2. **Verify Package Integrity with Hashing**

   ```sh
   ```

   ```sh
   sha256sum myapp.tar.gz
   ```

22.3 Summary

1. **Authentication** should use **password hashing, MFA, and OAuth2**.
2. **Encryption** is essential for **protecting data in transit and at rest**.

3. **Secure coding practices** prevent **SQL injection, XSS, and hardcoded secrets**.

4. **File permissions and API security** should be enforced to prevent unauthorized access.

5. **Logging and monitoring** are crucial for detecting security incidents.

6. **Code signing and integrity checks** protect against software tampering.

Next Chapter Preview: Deploying Cross-Platform Applications at Scale

1. Learn how to **deploy Python applications across cloud and local environments**.

2. Explore **CI/CD pipelines, Docker, and Kubernetes** for scalable deployments.

3. Implement **automatic updates and version control** for software distribution.

Chapter 23

Cross-Platform Testing Strategies

Testing is a crucial phase in software development, ensuring that an application functions correctly across **Windows, macOS, Linux, and mobile platforms**. Effective testing strategies help prevent **bugs, regressions, and compatibility issues**.

In this chapter, we will:

1. Explore **unit testing with `pytest` and `unittest`**.
2. Learn **automated UI testing** for desktop and mobile applications.

23.1 Unit Testing with pytest and unittest

I. Why Unit Testing?

Unit testing is a fundamental testing method that:

1. **Verifies individual functions and classes** for correctness.
2. **Prevents regressions** when modifying code.

3. **Ensures cross-platform consistency** in behavior.

Python has two primary frameworks for unit testing:

- unittest (built-in module).
- pytest (third-party, more powerful).

II. Using unittest: *The Built-In Python Testing Module*

1. Writing a Basic Unit Test

Create a file **test_math.py**:

```python
import unittest

def add(a, b):
    return a + b

class TestMathOperations(unittest.TestCase):
    def test_add(self):
        self.assertEqual(add(2, 3), 5)
        self.assertEqual(add(-1, 1), 0)
```

```
if __name__ == "__main__":
    unittest.main()
```

2. Running the Test

sh

```
python test_math.py
```

3. Advantages of unittest

Built into Python (no installation needed). Works on all platforms. Supports **test setup/teardown** with setUp() and tearDown().

III. Using pytest: *A More Powerful Testing Framework*

1. Installing pytest

sh

```
pip install pytest
```

2. Writing a Test with pytest

Modify **test_math.py** to:

```python
python

import pytest

def add(a, b):
    return a + b

def test_add():
    assert add(2, 3) == 5
    assert add(-1, 1) == 0
```

3. Running Tests with pytest

```sh
sh

pytest test_math.py
```

4. Advantages of pytest

More readable syntax (no need for classes).
Supports fixtures for better test setup.
Parallel test execution for large applications.

23.2 Automated UI Testing for Desktop and Mobile Apps

Automated UI testing ensures that graphical applications **work correctly across different operating systems and screen sizes**.

I. Testing GUI Applications with `PyTest` + `PyAutoGUI`

`PyAutoGUI` allows automated testing of desktop applications by simulating **mouse clicks and keystrokes**.

1. Installing PyAutoGUI

sh

```
pip install pyautogui
```

2. Writing a GUI Test

python

```
import pyautogui
import time

# Open Notepad (Windows)
pyautogui.hotkey("win", "r")
time.sleep(1)
```

```
pyautogui.write("notepad")
pyautogui.press("enter")

time.sleep(2)

# Type text in Notepad
pyautogui.write("Hello, automated UI testing!",
interval=0.1)

# Close Notepad
pyautogui.hotkey("alt", "f4")
pyautogui.press("enter")
```

Works on **Windows, macOS, and Linux**.
Automates **keyboard and mouse interactions**.
✖ **Limited to UI automation** (does not check underlying logic).

II. Testing Desktop Apps with pytest-qt *for PyQt Applications*

For PyQt-based desktop applications, use pytest-qt.

1. Installing pytest-qt

sh

```
pip install pytest-qt
```

2. Writing a PyQt UI Test

```
python
```

```python
from    PyQt6.QtWidgets    import    QApplication,
QPushButton
import pytest

@pytest.fixture
def app(qtbot):
    button = QPushButton("Click Me")
    qtbot.addWidget(button)
    return button

def test_button_click(app, qtbot):
    app.click()
    assert app.text() == "Clicked!"
```

Ideal for PyQt and PySide applications.
Can simulate UI interactions (button clicks, form inputs).

III. Automated Mobile UI Testing with Appium

For mobile applications, **Appium** allows testing on **Android and iOS**.

1. Installing Appium

sh

```
pip install Appium-Python-Client
```

2. Writing a Mobile UI Test (Android Example)

python

```
from appium import webdriver

capabilities = {
    "platformName": "Android",
    "deviceName": "emulator-5554",
    "app": "/path/to/app.apk"
}

driver                                    =
webdriver.Remote("http://localhost:4723/wd/hub"
, capabilities)
button                                    =
driver.find_element_by_accessibility_id("button
1")
button.click()
```

Works on **Android and iOS**. Supports **native, hybrid, and web apps**.

23.3 Summary

1. **Unit testing** ensures **code correctness across platforms**.

   o   Use `unittest` **(built-in)** for simple tests.

   o   Use `pytest` **(third-party)** for advanced features.

2. **Automated UI testing** verifies **graphical applications**.

   o   Use **PyAutoGUI** for desktop automation.

   o   Use **pytest-qt** for **PyQt applications**.

   o   Use **Appium** for **Android/iOS applications**.

Next Chapter Preview: Debugging and Profiling Python Applications

1. Learn **debugging techniques with pdb, PyCharm, and VSCode**.

2. Optimize performance using **profiling tools like cProfile and memory_profiler**.

3. Identify and fix **performance bottlenecks in Python applications**.

Chapter 24

Debugging Cross-Platform Applications

Debugging is an essential part of software development, especially for **cross-platform applications** that run on **Windows, macOS, Linux, and mobile devices**. Differences in system configurations, dependencies, and performance across operating systems make debugging more complex.

In this chapter, we will:

1. Explore **tools and techniques for debugging across multiple operating systems**.

2. Learn **remote debugging and effective logging strategies** for distributed applications.

24.1 Tools and Techniques for Debugging Across Operating Systems

I. Built-in Debugging with pdb *(Python Debugger)*

The Python **pdb module** is a built-in debugging tool that allows step-by-step execution and variable inspection.

1. Running a Script in Debug Mode

```python
python


import pdb


def divide(a, b):
    pdb.set_trace()   # Start debugging session
    return a / b


result = divide(10, 0)   # This will trigger a
ZeroDivisionError
```

2. Common pdb Commands

Command	Description
n (next)	Execute the next line of code.

Command	Description
`s` (step)	Step into a function call.
`c` (continue)	Continue execution until the next breakpoint.
`p variable`	Print the value of a variable.
`q` (quit)	Exit the debugger.

Cross-platform (works on all OS). **Lightweight and built into Python.** ✗ **Limited UI** (command-line only).

II. Debugging with IDEs (PyCharm, VSCode, WingIDE)

1. **PyCharm Debugger**
   - Provides **breakpoints, variable inspection, and step execution**.
   - Supports **remote debugging** for cloud and server applications.
2. **VSCode Debugger**
   - Works with **Windows, macOS, and Linux**.

    o   Supports **multi-threaded and Django application debugging.**

3. **WingIDE**

    o   Ideal for **embedded and scientific computing.**

    o   Supports **cross-platform remote debugging.**

Example: Adding a Breakpoint in VSCode

1. Open your Python script in VSCode.
2. Add a **breakpoint** by clicking next to the line number.
3. Press **F5** to start debugging.

Best for GUI-based debugging.

Great for complex applications.

✖ **Requires IDE installation.**

III. Debugging Python Applications with Logging

Logging is a **powerful alternative to print debugging** and allows for **persistent debugging records**.

1. Using Python's `logging` *Module*

```python
```

```python
import logging

# Configure logging
logging.basicConfig(
    filename="app.log",
    level=logging.DEBUG,
    format="%(asctime)s    -    %(levelname)s    -
%(message)s"
)

def divide(a, b):
    try:
        return a / b
    except ZeroDivisionError:
        logging.error("Attempted  to  divide  by
zero", exc_info=True)

result = divide(10, 0)
```

**Stores   error   logs   for   debugging   later.
Works across all platforms**.

24.2 Using Remote Debugging and Logging Effectively

I. Remote Debugging with debugpy (For Servers and Containers)

Use Case:

- When debugging applications running on **remote servers or containers**.
- Supports **Windows, macOS, Linux, and Docker**.

1. Installing debugpy

sh

```
pip install debugpy
```

2. Starting a Remote Debugging Session

python

```
import debugpy

# Listen on port 5678 for debugging
debugpy.listen(("0.0.0.0", 5678))

print("Waiting for debugger to attach...")
```

```
debugpy.wait_for_client()  # Wait for connection
before proceeding
```

```
print("Debugger attached!")
```

3. Connecting from VSCode (Client Machine)

1. Open **VSCode** and go to **Run > Add Configuration**.
2. Select **Python: Attach** and set the port to 5678.
3. Start debugging by pressing **F5**.

Debug servers and Docker containers remotely.
Works across all platforms.
✗ Requires additional setup.

II. Using Log Management Tools (For Distributed Applications)

For large applications, use centralized log management services such as:

Tool	Features
ELK Stack (Elasticsearch, Logstash, Kibana)	Cloud log monitoring
AWS CloudWatch	Remote logging for cloud apps
Splunk	Log analysis and monitoring
Fluentd	Lightweight log collection

1. Sending Logs to AWS CloudWatch

python

```
import boto3

client = boto3.client("logs")

client.put_log_events(
    logGroupName="MyAppLogs",
    logStreamName="AppStream",
    logEvents=[{"timestamp":        123456789,
"message": "Error detected"}]
)
```

**Centralized   log   monitoring.
Ideal for cloud-based applications.**

III. Debugging Memory and Performance Issues

1. Use `cProfile` for Performance Profiling

```python
python

import cProfile

def slow_function():
    total = sum(range(1000000))
    return total

cProfile.run("slow_function()")
```

Identifies slow parts of the code.

2. Use `memory_profiler` for Memory Debugging

```sh
sh

pip install memory_profiler
python

from memory_profiler import profile
```

```
@profile
def memory_test():
    data = [x for x in range(1000000)]
    return data


memory_test()
```

Detects memory leaks.

24.3 Summary

1. **Built-in tools** like pdb enable **step-by-step debugging**.
2. **IDEs like PyCharm and VSCode** provide **graphical debugging**.
3. **Logging with logging** is essential for **error tracking**.
4. **Remote debugging** with debugpy allows debugging of **servers and containers**.
5. **Performance profiling** with cProfile and memory_profiler helps detect **bottlenecks**.

Next Chapter Preview: Deploying Cross-Platform Applications at Scale

1. Deploy Python applications **on the cloud and on-premises**.
2. Use **Docker, Kubernetes, and CI/CD pipelines** for automation.
3. Implement **automatic updates and software distribution**.

Chapter 25

Emerging Trends in Cross-Platform Development

The landscape of **cross-platform Python development** is constantly evolving with new technologies and methodologies. Innovations such as **WebAssembly, cloud-based Python applications, and AI-powered development** are shaping the way Python is used across multiple platforms.

In this chapter, we will:

1. Explore **WebAssembly, cloud-based Python applications, and AI-driven development.**
2. Understand **how Python is evolving for multi-platform needs.**

26.1 The Rise of WebAssembly, Cloud-Based Python Apps, and AI-Powered Development

I. WebAssembly: Running Python in the Browser

1. **What is WebAssembly (WASM)?**
   - WebAssembly is a **binary instruction format** that enables high-performance applications to run in web browsers.
   - It allows **Python code to run in the browser**, eliminating the need for JavaScript.

2. **Python in WebAssembly: Pyodide and WASM Support**
   - **Pyodide** is a Python distribution compiled for WebAssembly, enabling Python execution in web applications.
   - **Example: Running Python in the Browser with Pyodide**

python

```
import pyodide
result = pyodide.eval_code("sum([1, 2, 3,
4, 5])")
print(result)   # Output: 15
```

3. **Advantages of WebAssembly for Python**

   i. Enables **cross-platform Python applications** in browsers.

   ii. No need for **server-side execution** (reduces cloud costs).

   iii. Improves **performance and security** compared to JavaScript-based solutions.

II. Cloud-Based Python Applications

1. **Shift to Cloud-First Python Development**

   o Python applications are increasingly being deployed as **serverless functions** or **cloud-native services**.

   o **Popular Cloud Services for Python**:

   i. **AWS Lambda** - Run Python scripts without managing infrastructure.

   ii. **Google Cloud Functions** - Serverless execution of Python functions.

    iii. **Azure Functions** - Integrate Python with Microsoft cloud services.

2. **Example: Deploying a Python Function to AWS Lambda**

python

```
import json

def lambda_handler(event, context):
    return {
        "statusCode": 200,
        "body": json.dumps("Hello from AWS Lambda!")
    }
```

3. **Advantages of Cloud-Based Python Development**

i. Reduces dependency on **device-specific execution**.

ii. Supports **real-time scaling** based on demand.

iii. Enables **cross-platform access from any device** with an internet connection.

III. AI-Powered Development in Python

1. **Python as the Leading AI and Machine Learning Language**
   - o Python is the primary language for AI development due to **libraries like TensorFlow, PyTorch, and Scikit-learn.**
   - o AI models can now be **optimized for cross-platform deployment** (e.g., AI on edge devices, mobile apps).

2. **AI-Assisted Code Generation**
   - o Tools like **GitHub Copilot** and **ChatGPT for Code** help developers **write and debug Python applications faster.**

3. **Example: Using AI-Powered Code Completion**

```python
from transformers import pipeline

generator = pipeline("text-generation", model="gpt-2")
result = generator("Write a Python function that calculates Fibonacci numbers:", max_length=100)
print(result)
```

4. **AI-Powered Debugging and Optimization**

o   AI is being used to **automatically detect bugs, suggest fixes, and optimize performance** in Python applications.

26.2 How Python is Evolving for Multi-Platform Needs

I. Python's Adaptability to Emerging Platforms

1. **Python for Edge Computing and IoT**
    o   Python is now being optimized for **low-power devices** in IoT and edge computing.
    o   **MicroPython** and **CircuitPython** allow Python to run on microcontrollers.

2. **Python for Mobile Development**
    o   Frameworks like **BeeWare and Kivy** are improving Python's presence in **native mobile development**.
    o   **Example: Deploying Python Apps to iOS and Android with BeeWare**

sh

```
briefcase create
briefcase build android
briefcase run android
```

II. The Role of Python in Quantum Computing

1. **Python as the Primary Language for Quantum Computing**

   o **IBM Qiskit** and **Google Cirq** are Python-based libraries for quantum computing.

   o **Quantum simulations can now be executed cross-platform** using cloud-based quantum processors.

2. **Example: Creating a Quantum Circuit with Qiskit**

```python
from qiskit import QuantumCircuit

qc = QuantumCircuit(2)
qc.h(0)
qc.cx(0, 1)
```

```
print(qc)
```

3. **How Quantum Computing Will Shape Cross-Platform Development**

i. Enables **high-performance computing** for cryptography and AI.

ii. Improves **scientific simulations** across different platforms.

iii. Expands Python's capabilities into **next-generation computing**.

26.3 Summary

1. **WebAssembly (WASM)** is enabling Python to run in web browsers.

2. **Cloud-based Python applications** are reducing platform dependency.

3. **AI-powered development** is making Python coding faster and more efficient.

4. **Python is expanding into edge computing, IoT, mobile, and quantum computing.**

Next Chapter Preview: Best Practices for Cross-Platform Python Development

1. Learn **best practices for writing maintainable, scalable, and portable Python applications.**
2. Explore **design patterns, modular programming, and testing methodologies.**
3. Implement **CI/CD pipelines for automated testing and deployment.**

Chapter 26

Final Thoughts and Next Steps

Cross-platform Python development has evolved significantly, enabling developers to build **efficient, scalable, and secure applications** across multiple environments, including **Windows, macOS, Linux, web, mobile, and embedded systems**. Throughout this book, we have explored a wide range of topics, from **foundational principles to advanced techniques**, covering **best practices for performance, security, and deployment**.

In this final chapter, we will:

1. Recap the key lessons learned throughout the book.
2. Provide resources for further learning and staying updated with Python trends.

27.1 Recap of Key Lessons Learned

I. Core Principles of Cross-Platform Development

1. **Portability and Compatibility**
   - o Python is inherently cross-platform but requires **careful handling of OS-specific behaviors**.
   - o Use **pathlib, os, and platform modules** to ensure compatibility.

2. **Writing Maintainable and Scalable Code**
   - o Follow **modular programming** and **design patterns** such as **MVC (Model-View-Controller)** and **Singleton**.
   - o Implement **unit tests and CI/CD pipelines** for code stability.

II. Key Technologies and Strategies

1. **Graphical User Interfaces (GUI)**
   - o Use **Tkinter, PyQt, Kivy, and BeeWare** for cross-platform desktop and mobile applications.

2. **Web Development and APIs**
   - o Python supports full-stack web development with **Flask, Django, and FastAPI**.
   - o **GraphQL and RESTful APIs** enhance interoperability between platforms.

3. **Mobile and Embedded Systems**

- o Mobile development is supported via **Kivy and BeeWare**, while **MicroPython and CircuitPython** enable IoT development.

4. **Cloud and Serverless Computing**

- o Python is widely used in **AWS, Azure, and Google Cloud** for serverless applications.

- o **Containers (Docker) and orchestration (Kubernetes)** enable scalable deployments.

5. **Security and Performance Optimization**

- o Implement **encryption (AES, bcrypt), secure authentication (OAuth2, JWT)**, and **logging**.

- o Optimize Python applications with **multiprocessing, threading, and asyncio**.

27.2 Resources for Further Learning and Staying Updated

I. Official Documentation and Learning Platforms

1. **Python Official Documentation** – https://docs.python.org/3/

2. **Real Python** – https://realpython.com/
3. **Full Stack Python** – https://www.fullstackpython.com/
4. **PyPI (Python Package Index)** – https://pypi.org/

II. Community and Open Source Contributions

1. **Python Enhancement Proposals (PEP)** – https://peps.python.org/
   - Keep track of changes in Python language features.
2. **GitHub Repositories for Python Projects** – https://github.com/topics/python
   - Contribute to open-source projects and learn best practices.
3. **Stack Overflow (Python Section)** – https://stackoverflow.com/questions/tagged/python
   - Find solutions to common problems and engage with the developer community.
4. **Reddit Python Community** – https://www.reddit.com/r/Python/
   - Discuss Python trends and new developments.

III. Conferences, Podcasts, and Online Courses

1. **PyCon (Python Conferences Worldwide)** – https://us.pycon.org/
   - o Attend **talks, workshops, and networking events**.
2. **Talk Python Podcast** – https://talkpython.fm/
   - o Covers **Python news, AI, web, and game development**.
3. **Coursera – Python for Everybody** – https://www.coursera.org/specializations/python
   - o Excellent course for **learning Python from scratch**.
4. **Udemy – Advanced Python Programming** – https://www.udemy.com/course/advanced-python-programming/
   - o Learn **advanced Python concepts like threading, async programming, and cloud deployment**.

IV. Staying Updated on Python Trends

1. **Follow Python's Roadmap** –
   https://devguide.python.org/
   - o Learn about upcoming Python versions and features.
2. **Join Python User Groups (PUGs)** –
   - o Find local meetups on https://www.meetup.com/topics/python/
3. **Subscribe to Python Weekly** –
   https://www.pythonweekly.com/
   - o Weekly updates on **libraries, articles, and job opportunities**.
4. **Monitor GitHub Trends** –
   https://github.com/trending/python
   - o Discover new Python projects gaining traction.

27.3 Next Steps in Your Python Journey

I. Choose a Path to Specialize In

1. **Web Development**

o   Master **Django, Flask, or FastAPI** for building scalable applications.

2. **Machine Learning and AI**

    o   Learn **TensorFlow, PyTorch, and Scikit-learn** for AI-powered solutions.

3. **Automation and DevOps**

    o   Use Python for **scripting, CI/CD, and cloud infrastructure automation**.

4. **Cybersecurity**

    o   Explore **ethical hacking, penetration testing, and security automation**.

II. Start a Python Project or Contribute to Open Source

1. Build a **personal project** to solidify knowledge.
2. Contribute to **open-source projects** on GitHub.
3. Develop a **Python library** or publish a package on PyPI.
4. Write **technical blogs** or create **video tutorials**.

III. Stay Engaged with the Python Community

1. Attend **conferences and workshops**.
2. Join **online discussions and forums**.
3. Network with **other developers and industry experts**.

27.4 Summary

1. Python's cross-platform capabilities make it one of the most versatile programming languages.
2. Mastering **testing, debugging, performance tuning, and deployment strategies** is essential.
3. Keeping up with **WebAssembly, cloud computing, and AI** ensures Python's relevance in emerging technologies.
4. Engaging with the **Python community and learning from open-source contributions** accelerates growth.
5. **Specializing in a specific domain**, whether web, AI, or automation, can boost career opportunities.

Final Words

This book has provided a **comprehensive guide** to mastering **cross-platform Python development**. The key to continued success is **constant learning, experimentation, and engagement with the developer community**.

Whether building **desktop applications, web services, AI-powered systems, or automation tools**, Python's flexibility makes it a powerful language for any **cross-platform development challenge**.

Where to Go Next?

1. **Experiment with real-world projects** to apply what you have learned.
2. **Stay updated with Python's roadmap and new frameworks.**
3. **Explore advanced topics like Rust-Python interoperability, AI-driven automation, and high-performance computing.**
4. **Share your knowledge** by teaching, blogging, or mentoring other developers.

www.ingramcontent.com/pod-product-compliance
Lightning Source LLC
LaVergne TN
LVHW022334060326
832902LV00022B/4041